THINK RICH

By H. Stanley Judd

THE CALIFORNIA WEIGHT LOSS PROGRAM

THINK

RICH

H. STANLEY JUDD

with ALVIN I. HAIMSON, Ph. D.
and FREDERICK D. SMITH

Delacorte Press/New York

Published by
Delacorte Press
1 Dag Hammarskjold Plaza
New York, N.Y. 10017

Manufactured in the United States of America

First printing

Designed by Leo McRee

Library of Congress Cataloging in Publication Data

Judd, H. Stanley.
Think rich.

Includes index.
1. Finance, Personal. I. Haimson, Alvin, I., joint author. II. Smith, Frederick D., joint author. III. Title.
HG179.J78 332'.024 78-3670
ISBN 0-440-08732-5

For Ingrid and Jennifer
with love

CONTENTS

INTRODUCTION

Money is a game with a lot of people out there spending millions of their dollars trying to get you to part with your own.

The average American family is overwhelmed with campaigns designed to motivate them to spend, spend, spend. Staffed by advertising agencies, marketing consultants, psychologists, aggressive professional managers, and highly paid salesmen, multimillion dollar corporations and government agencies work around the clock to persuade you and your family to part with *your* money.

How well you play the "money game" will to a great extent determine the kind of life you lead from now on. If you really play the game badly, it can lead to frustration, isolation, stress and a sea of debt.

No matter who you are, how much you make, or what goals you have for the rest of your life, you can learn the money management techniques contained in this 9-day program.

Even if you are dead broke, what you can learn from this

program can help you get back on your feet and keep from making the same money management mistakes the second time around.

If you have made a million, this program can still benefit you because the first five lessons deal with the psychology of managing money. All of us, almost from birth, develop thinking and behavior patterns relating to money. These patterns are deeply imprinted onto our "internal computer" and result in the way we think, act, and react to money.

If the right patterns have been imprinted onto our internal computer, we seem to go through life with financial ease, building up an estate, using money to get the things we want out of life. But if the wrong patterns have been imprinted, we often lead the up-and-down, frustrating life of someone who never seems to be able to get ahead of the game, who always seems swamped in a tide of unpaid bills.

The beautiful thing about money management is that anyone—anyone who can read and write—can master the money management techniques contained in this program.

You can learn how to win the money game for yourself and your family. You can start from where you are right now, *reprogram* your attitudes toward money, and immediately experience the relief of knowing that finally *you* are in control of your personal money management program.

So the next time a multimillion dollar corporation tries to play the supermarket game, the new car game, the loss-leader game, the home refinancing game, or any of the other games designed to lift money out of your pocket, you can tell them you're not going to play.

How much you make in your lifetime depends on a lot of things, some of which you control and some of which you don't. We don't know whether you will make a million dollars or not or even if you *want* to make a lot of money, but we do know if you aren't following the money management techniques outlined in this program, you are heading toward financial trouble. We can't tell you how much you'll make in your lifetime, but we can show you how to hang on to as much of it as you can along the way.

This program will show you how to learn to control money. Once you have learned this, you and your family can look forward to as much security, pleasure, fun, and peace of mind as anyone can expect in this world.

What more could anyone want?

LESSON 1

UNDERSTANDING YOURSELF

> **As you cannot do what you wish, you should wish for what you can do.**
>
> **—Terence**

Before you can begin to understand how to use money, what it is, or how it works, you've got to know where you are. What are your attitudes, good or bad, right or wrong, toward money? How are you using money now? What fears do you have about money? What insecurities? In what ways do you handle money well?

Whenever you learn a new process you have to determine your current skill level. An athlete, for example, who works out every day and is in top physical shape, begins learning tennis at a much higher level of proficiency than a middle-aged, overweight person who hasn't exercised in years.

Once you have evaluated your own attitudes toward money (through using the Personality Profile) and determined objectively how good or bad a money manager you really are, you can then begin to improve your skills.

A review of your present financial situation gives you your starting place—where you are now. The changes you will have to make (through reprogramming) depend on how far you have come and how far you want to go.

After you become aware of your present behavior and thinking patterns about money, you can then begin to develop your new money management strategy. By completing this first step you will be on your way toward becoming a more skilled money manager.

Most other money management books take the position that money is "out there" somewhere—something hard, real, which is managed through various manipulative techniques.

We don't agree!

Money is part of an organic experience. In itself, money has no value—it is *relative.* Its value to you depends entirely upon who you are, what you want, and how far you are from where you want to be.

Other money management programs often fail because they throw a reader into a sea of financial terms (cash flow, depreciation, tax shelter, balance sheet, assets, investments, interest return, etc.) without taking into account the psychological attitudes a person has toward money. Widow, teen-ager, and business executive alike are all introduced to money management as if they start out on the same level.

Before you can learn to manage money successfully, you first have to take a hard look at the way you perceive it.

Therefore, this lesson deals with a practical method you can use to evaluate yourself objectively: to see what, if any, childhood hang-ups you may still have about money and to begin to look at money in a new way and achieve new insights into money.

Successful money management requires that you be skilled in three key areas:

1. SELF-AWARENESS—being able to see what is really happening in your life, not what you wish would happen or would like to see happen or don't want to admit *is* happening.
2. AWARENESS OF/SENSITIVITY TO OTHER PEOPLE—being able to anticipate how other people will act in a given circumstance, not how you would like them to act, hope they will act, or fear they will act.
3. UNDERSTANDING HOW MONEY WORKS—being able to *predict* how money will flow in transactions between yourself and other people.

In this lesson you will learn what you need to know about yourself in order to manage your money successfully from now on.

YOU ARE RESPONSIBLE

It is futile to start out trying to learn the mechanics of managing money if your "head isn't together."

If you are disorganized, often disoriented, a sporadic record-keeper, and not even interested enough to learn how to balance your checkbook, you are going to be a lousy money manager.

So your first important step is to take a good, long look at how you operate on a daily basis.

What happens to your money reflects your particular state of mind and organizational skills. True, you can employ someone to keep your records for you (an accountant, a CPA, a money manager), but you can never employ someone to take the responsibility of managing your money. *You are responsible.*

If you want to become a successful money manager,

you've got to organize your thinking about money and your handling of it. This doesn't mean you have to take the fun out of your life or spend all of your time keeping records and filing receipts.

What it does mean is that you are going to have to think creatively and consistently about how you plan to use money from now on.

MONEY IS NEUTRAL

The reason people have sought wealth for so long is that money doesn't take sides. Money is a power that does not discriminate between people. Other sources of power often depend on your relationship with someone else. Political power, social power, management power—each of these depends on your being able to work with other people successfully.

Money is really beautiful. It can create instant power for anyone who has it. But unfortunately, few people realize this and often fail to take advantage of it when they do come into a surplus amount of money.

This is why so many young entrepreneurs, who "come up fast" and become almost instant millionaires, often go back down into bankruptcy or substantial debt just as fast.

Remember that using money is a *process,* a skill you can learn just as you learned to drive a car or operate your new pocket calculator.

Learn to use money well and it works for you; use it badly and you end up working for it . . . not really being on top of your own resources.

MONEY HANG-UPS FROM YOUR PAST

Just as you carry around with you in your internal computer thinking and behavior patterns about food, people, your own self-image, friendship, your community, and your world, you also carry around very specific patterns about money.

These past experiences have created your "money style." Though you may not be aware of it, you have developed an automatic money style, which defines to a great extent the amount of money you are making now and the amount of money you will continue to make until you change your patterns.

What patterns do you presently carry around in your internal computer? By using the Personality Profile in this program, you will be able to see where you are at right now in relation to money. You will find out whether you have a poverty attitude, a clerk's attitude, a middle-income attitude, an executive's attitude, an entrepreneur's attitude, or a millionaire's attitude toward money. You will find out whether you are afraid of money or have a positive, aggressive attitude toward it.

It is vital that you become aware of your money attitude. Unless you do, you will probably go through life frustrated, because your money desires will always exceed your money potential. Or if you do find a way to earn all the money you need, you really won't understand how you did it or why it happened. In other words, you must *understand* money before you can really use it effectively.

WHY MOST PEOPLE NEVER MAKE ANY REAL MONEY

Most of us who have not grown up in wealthy families have a middle-income attitude toward money. This middle-income attitude keeps us generally afloat in society but rarely allows us to develop the skills to make a fortune.

There is nothing wrong with having a middle-income attitude if you want it, but if you aren't really satisfied with living a middle-income life, you will lose your opportunity to live the alternative life-style you might really enjoy.

No matter how many schemes you may try out to earn more money, you will probably not do so until you have raised your money attitude from a middle-income attitude to an executive's attitude or a millionaire's attitude.

This is true because psychologically we generally tend to live the lives we *expect* to live. This means we continually return to a life-style that demonstrates we are what we really believe we are. Thus, the middle-income-attitude person who suddenly strikes it rich usually ends up returning to a middle-income life-style, unless he or she changes, or re-programs, this middle-income attitude into a new attitude.

So right now, you are probably right where you expect yourself to be. And that's very good, because once you become aware of this you can open up your life by developing whatever attitude you might like to have.

AWARENESS—IT REALLY WORKS

Once you get rid of the various negative attitudes toward money (e.g., that someone else has the power to determine whether you will make more money or not, that you are now poor because you were born poor, that making money depends on luck or getting the breaks, or that there is a conspiracy of wealthy people or international corporations trying to keep you from making a lot of money) then you can apply your energy to making the kind of money you want to make.

In other words, by becoming aware of the fact that you alone determine your own potential, you have reached the first step toward becoming someone with potential to make more money. This doesn't guarantee that you will do so. You may not really want it once you discover how much you will have to pay to make more of it. You may discover that it will take just too much effort to begin all over again. But even so, you will be in a better position to live the life you are now living, because you will understand the money management process.

IT'S OK TO BE POOR IF YOU REALLY WANT TO BE

Once *you* take responsibility for yourself and your own actions, you don't have to worry or care anymore what other people think you should do or be. You can be what you damn well want to be. There's a big, wide world out there with all kinds of adventures and opportunities, and you can take advantage of them or leave them alone if you want to.

This freedom of thinking is the beginning of putting your life together your way. And until you get to this level of awareness you will probably not be able to manage your money successfully, because you will always be playing somebody else's game.

You can never really win a game until you play your own game—a game in which you determine the rules and control how you are going to win it.

USING MONEY AS AN EXCUSE

People who "don't have it together" and who aren't taking responsibility for themselves often lay off their trips on money: "I could have been something better if only we hadn't been poor"; "I've never gotten ahead because I never could get enough money together"; "If only my family had been rich, I would have been successful."

Money gets the rap for just about every failure in life. It is an easy way to avoid reality. The "no money" or "poverty" excuse takes all the responsibility off the individual where it belongs and puts it "out there" on the rest of society.

This attitude keeps people precisely where they feel comfortable, not comfortable because they like where they are (on the contrary, they may intensely dislike where they are), but comfortable because they are in familiar territory and they understand *they are where they expect to be* but most likely don't know how to change.

THE SIX PRINCIPAL MONEY ATTITUDES

Most of us never fit entirely into one specific money attitude. However, it is useful to know the six general categories into which most of us place ourselves from time to time. The following six money attitudes are generalized to give you an idea of the usual results that follow if you select one of these money attitudes as your own.

1. THE POVERTY ATTITUDE:

This person really believes that his or her life is lived in poverty and will never change. The poverty attitude encourages a state of hopelessness, depression, and dependence. The poverty attitude usually throws all responsibility on someone else (the state, the nation, etc.) for the continued survival of the individual who has taken this attitude toward money.

RESULTS:

A person with a poverty attitude rarely manages money successfully. Usually, there is little or no money to manage and the person's energy is spent dealing with the bureaucracy that has to assume responsibility for his or her survival. The world now owes the person with a poverty attitude a living. Personal initiative has been stifled and smothered. Escape often takes the form of excessive eating, drinking, use of drugs, violence, or TV watching.

2. THE CLERK'S ATTITUDE:

A step up from the poverty attitude is the clerk's attitude. People with this attitude hold down jobs which are usually routine and relatively easy to do. This attitude encourages people to seek job security, take few risks, and stay in the same place. People with this attitude are usually afraid they may lose their job. They may believe that whoever they work for owes them a paycheck no matter what the quality of their performance. These people are stuck in a money attitude not quite as damaging as the poverty attitude but every bit as restrictive.

RESULTS:

The clerk's attitude tends to restrict personal initiative and inhibit personal growth. Since people with this attitude are just "hanging on" and going no place, they often become bitter and depressed about life. Unlike people who really *enjoy* the work which is routine at the clerk's level, people with the *clerk's attitude* toward money rarely enjoy their work because they feel life has passed them by. They are "punching in and out of work" with no hope that things will ever change for them in the future. They mainly look forward to retirement only to find that the limited surplus money, which this attitude enables them to save, hardly allows them to survive.

3. THE MIDDLE-INCOME ATTITUDE:

A middle-income attitude toward money is a healthy attitude which accepts reality and allows the individual to perform in a positive way and to experience continued growth throughout life. Most of us are middle-income wage earners. It is the existence of the middle-income family that has enabled this country to survive with the maximum amount of freedom and growth. However, the person with a middle-income attitude toward money who really desires to make more money often faces a frustrating and bitter series of experiences.

This is true because the middle-income attitude is a conservative attitude toward money, which does not prepare the individual to take the kinds of risks that must be taken to move to a higher level of money awareness and income. People with a middle-income attitude who are always trying to get rich usually end up spending their money for mail order schemes or other "ideas" but rarely make any real money.

RESULTS:

People who enjoy what they are doing can use the middle-income attitude to make an excellent life for themselves and their children. Conservative money management strategies can salt away enough capital to provide for retirement. Usually the work middle-income people do is vital to the continued success of our economy. Often, though annual income may be relatively low, the middle-income person is able to have much more free time to use. This opens a wide range of exciting and fulfilling opportunities for personal growth and development.

4. THE EXECUTIVE'S ATTITUDE:

A step above the middle-income attitude is the executive's attitude. This attitude is the middle-income attitude raised to a higher level. Instead of wanting to make $18,000 a year, the executive aims at $45,000 or $125,000.

A person with the executive's attitude understands the way our economy works and takes time to learn skills necessary to earn more money.

People with this attitude are usually good at taking risks within their skill area but often bad at taking risks with their own money. Basically, the executive is someone with a middle-income attitude toward money who has raised the level of income he or she earns.

RESULTS:

People with the executive attitude usually do very well filling the needs our society has for leaders and people with special skills not easily duplicated. These people assume tremendous responsibility and are paid for doing so. As long as these people concentrate their efforts on what they know how to do, they continue to grow and develop.

However, when people with this attitude attempt to go out and make a lot of money, they fall on their face and lose a lot of money. For one reason, they are usually too busy with their own work to be able to spend the personal energy it takes to become an entrepreneur.

5. THE ENTREPRENEUR'S ATTITUDE:

It is this attitude that creates the great wealth in our society. The entrepreneur becomes a money professional, who looks through money to precise objectives. The entrepreneur spends enormous energy concentrating on achieving an objective (often having to sacrifice the normal relationships and pleasures the rest of us place first on our list of priorities).

Just as there are a few athletes who become champions, there are a few people in each generation who become entrepreneurs. These people create the new businesses, which at tremendous risk provide new services for which they are extremely well rewarded.

RESULTS:

Few of us have the temperament, the drive, the ambition, and the persistence to become successful entrepreneurs. For those who do, life often offers the unique rewards reserved for exceptional people who are able to live life on their own terms. Their lives tend to be rich with experience and adventure and the reward of creating something that provides a benefit to many other people.

6. THE MILLIONAIRE'S ATTITUDE:

This is the attitude we can all have toward money no matter how little or how much money we have. This is the attitude that frees us from money and allows us to experience the rich rewards our highly technological society offers. It is the attitude that puts money in its place and concentrates our efforts on the real stuff of life. The person with this attitude usually glows with life and finds more than enough to keep busy for a lifetime.

RESULTS:

This attitude is so important that you will spend Lesson 3 learning how to master it for yourself. The pleasure it can bring to your life is unlimited. The freedom it brings is sweet and wonderful.

Most important, it is not restricted to people who already have money or the skills to earn a lot of money. Each of us, whoever we are and whatever our circumstances, can develop this attitude toward money and use it to get the things out of life we want for ourselves.

KEY POINT

Your attitude toward money determines the amount of money you can expect to manage. Usually you will return to the money level you expect. That's why no matter how rich some people may become, if they retain the poverty attitude toward money they end up broke.

THE PERSONALITY PROFILE:

Turn now to Section 1 of the Personality Profile on the next page. Take as much time as you need to fill it out. Spend the rest of the day thinking about the attitudes you have toward money, for you will only really become a successful money manager after you understand the importance of your money attitude and how it affects your life.

DO NOT GO ON TO LESSON 2 UNTIL TOMORROW.

PERSONALITY PROFILE

SECTION 1 UNDERSTANDING YOURSELF

NAME ______________________ AGE ____________
OCCUPATION ______________ EDUCATION__________
MARRIED _____ SINGLE _____ DIVORCED __________
NO. OF CHILDREN ______________________________
HEIGHT ____ WEIGHT ____ PHYSICAL CONDITION ____
HOBBIES/INTERESTS ____________________________
____
ANY MAJOR ILLNESS DURING LAST YEAR__________
BEST FRIEND OUTSIDE FAMILY ___________________

1. How do you normally feel?

__Excited by life	__Secure
__Dull	__Hemmed in
__Anxious	__Relaxed
__Overworked	__Young
__Joyful	__Happy
__Positive	__Content
__Optimistic	__Old
__Confident	__Successful
__Afraid	__Going nowhere
__Alert, curious	__In love with life
__Bored by life	__Hopeful
__Vigorous, healthy	__At peace with the world
__Sick	__Insecure

2. Are you generally optimistic about your future? (If not,

why?) ____________________

____

3. Are you happy with your present career? ________
4. Are there any major personal problems you are finding it difficult to cope with? ____________________

____

5. Do you like yourself? (If not, what don't you like?) ____

____

6. Do you have any of the following fears?

__Fear of poverty
__Fear of losing a friend, child, loved one
__Fear of growing old
__Fear of sickness
__Fear of strangers
__Fear of failure
__Fear of death
__Fear of losing youth
__Fear of pain
__Fear of losing your job

7. Is there anyone who doesn't like you? ________

____

Why? ____________________

8. What are your friends like? Do they have money problems too?

____

9. Do you feel trapped by life? ____________
10. Is your marriage satisfying? ____________
11. Is your life exciting? ____________
12. Can you think of any major frustrations you may have?

____

13. When you need answers, do you feel OK about asking someone else for help or do you think you ought to figure out the answers yourself? ____________
14. Do you tend to wait to see what other people want you to do before you act or do you jump into situations and see what happens? ____________
15. Do you believe you know how to make things happen in your life the way you want them to happen? ______
16. If you could change just one thing about you what would it be? ____________

Why? ____________________

17. What do you think other people say is your best quality? _________ Why? ________________________
18. Are you the type of person who likes lots of projects going or do you prefer to have things happen one at a time? ____
19. Do you like to take risks? __________ Why? __________
20. What is the general limit of your risk-taking behavior?

____

21. Do you get tense and nervous inside when you are confronted with a new situation? _________ Why? __
22. Do you tend to take good care of yourself physically?
    - __Do you get some exercise every day?
    - __Do you eat a well-balanced diet?
    - __Do you avoid overeating?
    - __Do you eat a lot of sugars or starches?
    - __Do you drink a lot of coffee?
    - __Are you a heavy drinker?
    - __Are you addicted to any other drugs?
23. When was the last time you had a complete physical exam? ____
24. How much time do you spend thinking about how you are feeling? ______ Do you tend to talk with others about your feelings or do you keep your thoughts to yourself? ____
25. Do you usually react to a crisis situation in your life or do you plan ahead to organize your activities? ______
26. How much time do you spend taking care of the material things in your life? __________________________
27. Do you like to be around a lot of people or just a few people at a time? __________________________________
28. Which describes your reaction to people in positions of authority?

__Comfortable	__Friendly
__Afraid	__Cautious
__Carefree	__Resentful
__Quiet	__Anxious to talk to them

29. Is money important to you? _________ Why? _______
30. Do you wish you had more money to spend?_______
31. Why do you feel you need more money?__________
32. Does having money give you a sense of security/power? _________ If so, why? ______________
33. Are you using "not having enough money" as an excuse to avoid trying new experiences? _________ If so, why? ____
34. What is it you don't have that you think money will bring you?______________________________________
35. How much money would/do you feel comfortable spending at one time? _______________________
36. What do you like to spend money for?
    __Entertainment
    __Clothing
    __Escape
    __On other people
    __Food
    __Only necessities
    __Expenses
37. On what do you least like to spend money? _______ _________ Why? ____________________________
38. What rewards do you now get from spending money?
    __I spend money when I'm nervous and it relaxes me.
    __I spend money when I'm unhappy and it makes me feel better.
    __I spend money when I'm frustrated or angry and it releases the tension.
    __I can't resist spending money whenever I have some.
    __I almost never spend money on myself.
    __It gives me a sense of power to spend money.
    __It gives me a sense of security to spend money paying my bills because then I have nothing hanging over my head.
    __I like to spend money on other people because it makes me feel I have helped them in some way.

__I like to spend money because it makes me feel I'm OK. People won't think I'm a miser hoarding my money.
__I think it's a good idea to keep the economy going by spending my money. It's part of good business and I'm doing my part when I spend it.

39. What rewards do you get for not spending money?
__I feel secure that I'll have plenty of money left over for the future.
__I want others to participate in making things happen so I don't spend a lot.
__I work hard for my money and don't feel like letting it go. I like to make it last.
__I feel that if I'm careful about spending money I will be able to accumulate it for savings and investments.
__I feel people will respect me if I'm careful with my money.
__I feel I'm helping other people in my family by controlling my spending.
__I like to think I'm a frugal person.
__I was told it is a good idea to save money though I don't really understand why.
__It gives me a sense of power to have more money than my family and friends have.

40. Are you generally afraid of what the future will bring as far as your finances are concerned? __________ If so, why? ______________________________

41. How would you rate your money managing skills?
__Poor __Fair __Good __Excellent

42. Did your parents discuss money matters with you when you were a child? __________ If so, how did it make you feel? __Good __Frightened __Angry __Happy __Secure __Insecure __Energetic __Ashamed

43. What people do you feel comfortable or uncomfortable

with when the subject of money is being talked about?
__Your family __Your employer __Your banker __Your attorney __Your friends __Clerks in stores __Teachers __Other

44. What/how do you feel when you lose some money?
I feel ____________________

____

45. How much money do you feel it is OK to lose?
$1–$5 ____________________
$10–$25 ____________________
$25–$50 ____________________
$50–$100 ____________________
Over $100 __________ Explain __________

46. When you have lost money did you tell anyone?
Yes __________ No __________ If no, why not? __________ If yes, why? __________

47. Which major money attitude do you believe you have right now? Be honest!
__The poverty attitude
__The clerk's attitude
__The middle-income attitude
__The executive's attitude
__The entrepreneur's attitude
__The millionaire's attitude

HOW TO EVALUATE YOUR PERSONALITY PROFILE

It is important for you to use your Personality Profile information as a basis for your thinking about yourself, about money, and about changes you may want to make in your life. These questions should trigger a new awareness on your part.

For this reason we have not included a rating (e.g., how do you rate yourself from 1 to 10) at the end of each

Personality Profile section. Your objective is not to find out whether you are the best or worst money manager in the world but rather to become aware of your own level of money management competence. If you like the idea of scoring yourself, look to your results rather than the answers you come up with when you fill out your Personality Profile.

This Personality Profile is only a beginning. Hopefully, it will start you thinking objectively about yourself. It will get you in the habit of asking yourself questions like: Hey, what's really happening here? Am I really following the right money management strategy? Is it possible my thinking about this is wrong? Am I doing what's right for me?

LESSON 2

UNDERSTANDING MONEY

Money is a good servant but a bad master.
—Bacon

Your second step to successful money management is to understand how money really works, what it is, and how you can use it to get what you want from life.

Since money is a resource each of us uses and needs in a different way, your definition of the role money will play in your life depends upon the kind of life you decide to lead. Money is a relative resource—it has different values for different people.

Money has very definite laws and works the same way no matter who uses it. Money is neutral. It is predictable. In a short period of time, you can learn the fundamentals of money management and demonstrate to yourself the real control you can have over it in your life.

After you understand money, you can then align your needs to your money resources to develop a strategy to achieve your personal goals. You can learn effective techniques which will be of tremendous value no matter how much or how little money you intend to manage.

One of the most important emotions you will be able to learn to avoid in your daily life is *fear* of money. Most of us fear money because we don't understand it; we don't understand how to get enough of it to meet our perceived needs. Once we understand money, we can then design our own money plan that will *work.* Understanding money opens doors of opportunity to you, but more important, it gives you a new personal security which goes far beyond the amount of money you do or do not have right now.

In this lesson you are going to learn how money works. You will learn the key point that money is *relative.* Money works differently in large amounts than in small ones. Understanding this relative theory of money will enable you to achieve your specific short- and long-term financial goals.

Once you understand the "money process," you can begin to see what you have been doing right and wrong. You will learn how to play the money game and win.

This lesson reviews the principal "money laws," which determine how money works. You are given the rules of the money game. You learn the three key positions you will be in at any given time:

The minus (−) position
The even (0) position
The plus (+) position

WHAT MONEY REALLY IS

In Lesson 1, you learned how important your own perception of yourself is in relation to how you will use money in your life. In this lesson, we are going to take a look at the other side of money—money as it operates outside of yourself.

Just as you spent the first lesson looking inward at yourself, spend this lesson looking at money from the outside. Look at it as if you were standing outside our society observing it from a spaceship, from another planet. This is important because you must learn to shed your emotional attitudes toward money before you can really learn how to use it effectively.

Right now you have all sorts of attitudes toward money, which add up to your major money thinking and behavior patterns. In this lesson try to get around these attitudes so that you can see money in operation without having your own personal thinking about it warp what you see.

In order to get yourself psychologically positioned for this lesson, pretend that you are somewhere out in the future, 500 or 600 years, looking back at this period in a history class. You are interested in finding out how these primitives used their money.

The first thing that would strike you is that you see less and less money with each passing month. True, from time to time, you see someone reach into a wallet or purse and take out some paper or coins and give them to someone else for some service or purchase. But more and more, you see people merely handing plastic cards back and forth, writing checks once a month, and looking over computer printouts.

Money today is no more than a substitute for a particular level of personal resources, a symbol used to make it easier to take from and give to society the things people trade in.

Money is a *convenience.* Without it, our highly technological system simply wouldn't work. A system of money sustains the process through which value is earned by one person who provides a service or product for which one or more other people are willing to pay. Our society works by fulfilling needs. When there are no more needs to fulfill, new needs are invented or contrived.

This is a totally objective process. This is good because

it allows each person to select areas in which he or she wants to provide a service.

IT TAKES TWO TO MAKE MONEY WORK

Unless a person has at least one other person to trade with, money has no value at all. Value is only created in money when there is something to buy or sell. Even here, the value does not come from the money itself but from what there is to buy or sell. In other words, to use money successfully a person has to look through it to the services and products it represents.

Values are changing constantly. So there is no absolute value to anything. A good crop generally lowers prices of food (unless the government pays to plow under the surplus or the farmer holds it back to keep prices up). But even this does not always keep the value of a product stable. When sugar prices, for example, went too high people simply stopped buying sugar and switched to substitutes. Prices tumbled.

The value of the money itself depends on the faith everyone has in the currency. When nations are unable to supply products people need or want, currencies inflate until sometimes no one will accept it for the things they want to sell. Substitute money is instantly created: for example, cigarettes after the end of the Second World War.

This is important to understand because this means a person has tremendous control over the value of money as it relates to his or her life. A person is rarely in a position to control the value of the nation's currency but is always in absolute control over the value of money as it relates to his or her life.

This is true because the value of money depends on the

things a person believes he or she *needs* to buy. The more expensive the needs, the less value money has (because the person is going to have to spend more of it).

KEY POINT

> Reflect on this basic principle until you really understand it. It is not the world out there that determines your money needs, it is *you* and you alone who does so.
>
> Once you understand this, you will have learned a powerful principle you can then use to learn to master control over money.
>
> To sum up, you are playing a game against everyone else. You are buying and selling things you have in your account. You are setting up your game. If you set it up right, you are going to win it. If you set it up wrong or let someone else set you up, you are going to lose it.

THE RELATIVITY OF MONEY

Let's get back to your spaceship in the future and observe once again what is going on down here right now.

What you are seeing is a lot of people doing all sorts of things in relation to money. They spend time earning money by convincing someone else what they do is worth paying them to do it. They are spending money they earn buying things they want or need.

There are a limited amount of resources available which all these people use. Some use these resources well and prosper, other use them poorly and do not.

None of these activities really relates to money itself. They relate to the things that money buys.

THE THREE MONEY SITUATIONS

All these people are going to be in one of three positions in relation to the value of what they have to buy and sell vis-à-vis what other people have to buy and sell.

1. Some will be in a minus (−) position. This means that they are in debt to other people. They have bought more than they have sold and are surviving on credit. In other words, someone else with a surplus of value in his account is supporting the person in the minus (−) position.

The minus (−) position is the most risky position to be in. It is important not to confuse the minus (−) position with "borrowing." You may be in debt because you bought a house and mortgaged it to the bank. However, if the value of the house equals or is more than the amount you owe on the house, you are not in a minus (−) position.

There are people who have millions of dollars of debt but are in a plus (+) position, because the value of the resources they own is far greater than the amount of debt they have.

The minus (−) position means that these people are not able to afford the debt they are carrying. Each month, they slip a little further behind until, finally, they are forced into bankruptcy or some other means of restructuring their finances.

2. The even (0) position. Most Americans are in the even (0) position. This means that if you add up everything you own that you could sell (assets) and sold it all, you would just pay off all your debts (liabilities). The even (0) position is dangerous, because a person is not protected against a financial crisis situation, such as loss of job or ill health.

3. The plus (+) position. People in the plus (+) position have accumulated values of one kind or another that are greater than their debts or liabilities. If they had to sell everything, they would come out ahead and be left with surplus value or *capital.*

The plus (+) position is the best possible position to be in, because it provides sufficient resources to cover ongoing costs while providing a cushion for emergencies.

KEY POINT

> This is the basic way money operates in our society. And you don't need to go through an elaborate process to know where you are. Chances are you understand exactly which of the three positions you and your family are in right now.

MONEY DOESN'T CARE ABOUT YOUR PROBLEMS

It is important to remember that since we are looking at a process, what happened in the past or what might happen in the future doesn't really matter. The farmer who has worked hard all his life and provided excellent services to others is suddenly ruined by a three-year drought. The farm is sold and the farmer is left with no resources. In spite of the fact that the farmer has been an excellent member of society, the farmer is now in a minus (−) position. The farmer, in order to survive, must use a strategy appropriate to the minus (−) situation. He must find a job or discover another way to earn the income it will take to support him and his family.

KEY POINT

> Most people do not accept this fact about money: They don't want to accept the "neutrality" of money, the fact that money doesn't care about their problems. They wish or hope that what happened to them in the past will protect them in the future. They feel they have earned the right to continue to live the kind of life they have lived in the past even though their source of income may have dried up. Because of this, many people do not move quickly enough to change their strategies when they are suddenly moved from a plus (+) or even (0) position into a minus (−) position. In many cases, assets which could have supported them are eventually lost, because they tried to live as if they were in a plus (+) position when they were not.

Many people find this process cruel and heartless, and perhaps it is. On the other hand, since there are methods most of us can use to move from a minus (−) position into a plus (+) position, it is not so cruel as it might appear.

Because the process is neutral, it does not protect those who in the past (through inheritance or hard work) were in the plus (+) position but for one reason or another have now moved into a minus (−) position.

This gives everyone a chance to play the money game.

WHAT SECURITY REALLY MEANS

The ultimate security is your understanding of reality. Insecurity results from believing in something that isn't true and trying to force your opinion onto reality. Since your opinion is unrealistic you are insecure, because in spite of the fact that you may consciously fool yourself into believing you are right, your inner computer "knows" you are doomed to fail in the end.

When you accept the reality of your situation, you can then start to work to achieve your objectives realistically. You will no longer be insecure, because you know where reality is and what you have to do to survive. If you are poor, you are poor and you must start from there, admitting it. You then adopt strategies for moving out of poverty.

Insecurity, then, is a state of mind or an attitude that isn't working. Security is a thinking or behavior pattern that *is* working.

SUMMARY

The money process is neutral. People in the plus (+) position benefit most from the process. People in the minus (−) position benefit the least. Once you understand this, you can select the money style you want and plan your activities toward achieving your goals. Unless you are willing to accept the reality of the neutrality of money (i.e., nobody "owes" anybody anything) you will probably never be able to become a successful money manager.

You begin to become a successful money manager when you understand the rules of the money game and accept absolutely where you are right now . . . where you are starting from.

You are broke? Bankrupt? Down and out? Don't lose hope! Millions of other people have picked themselves up and fought their way back into a plus (+) position. John D. Rockefeller was broke as was Henry Ford, Andrew Carnegie, and many other people who went on to become millionaires.

WHAT YOU CAN DO TO GET FREE OF MONEY

Fortunately, you have the option of defusing money of its power over you if you decide you want to do so. This means that no matter what your financial situation at the moment (poor, middle-income, rich, etc.), you can free yourself of the negative stresses or power this situation has over your physical and mental health and use your new money attitude to start playing the money game your way. We call this the millionaire's attitude, and we will spend the next lesson defining it and showing you how you can use it successfully.

THE PERSONALITY PROFILE:

Turn to Section 2 of the Personality Profile. Take no more than twenty minutes to fill it out. Spend the rest of the day thinking about how money works "out there" in the world. Try to remove the attitudes you have had toward money or the emotions you may feel about money and observe how it works as if you were looking down from a spaceship in outer space. If you were learning to play tennis, you would observe tennis players to see how they played the game. Do the same thing now with money. See if you can begin to get insights into how money works . . . insights you haven't perhaps seen yet, because you have been too emotionally involved.

DO NOT GO ON TO LESSON 3 UNTIL TOMORROW.

PERSONALITY PROFILE

SECTION 2
UNDERSTANDING MONEY

1. Do you feel you understand how money works in this country? ___________ If not, why not? ___________
2. Do you fear inflation? __________ Why? ___________
3. Do you understand how inflation works? ___________
4. Do you understand how the federal government controls the money supply? ___________
5. Do you think someone is out there trying to take your money away from you? __________ If so, why? ______
6. Do you feel we are heading for a collapse of the economy, as in 1929? __________ If so, why? ___________
7. Do you believe that everyone can get rich if they are willing to work at it? __________ If not, why not? ____
8. Do you want to be a capitalist? __________ If not, why not? ___________
9. Do you believe the government owes every citizen a minimum standard of living? ______ If so, why? ______
10. Do you understand thoroughly:
    - __How banks rent money?
    - __How the stock market works?
    - __How the commodity market works?
    - __How the present tax system works?
    - __How the real-estate market works?
    - __How the bond market works?
    - __How to set up a new business?
    - __None of the above. If so, why? ___________

11. What money-earning skills have you learned? ________

____

12. How do you spend your free time?

    __Learning new money-earning skills
    __Starting up a new business
    __Investing your money
    __Watching TV
    __Playing golf, tennis, etc.
    __With friends
    __Shopping
    __Escaping
    __Other

13. If you are not spending your free time learning how to earn more money, why aren't you? ____________

14. Do you feel you know how money works in your family? Who controls the flow of money? What are the attitudes about money in your family? ____________

15. What are the three things that characterize your ability to earn more money in the general marketplace? What affects the amount of money you make?

    1. ______________________________
    2. ______________________________
    3. ______________________________

16. Who controls the ultimate amount of money in your life?

    __Your job source
    __Your spouse (If so, why?)
    __The IRS
    __The economy in general
    __I do

17. What role does the bank or savings and loan company play in relation to the money you have in your life?

    __They are the ones who let me have money when I need it.
    __They are the ones who keep my money for me and give me some interest for it.
    __They are the people who keep me from getting

very much money unless I really need it and can justify my needs.
__They are friends of mine who are concerned about how I am doing with my money.
__If I'm careful and reliable, I can arrange to borrow money from them if I need it.
__They are in the business of renting out my money and I can get it from them when I'm willing to pay the fees.
__If they don't give me a good rate, I can go to another bank and make a better deal.

18. When you walk into a bank are you a bit nervous and cautious? ______ If so, why? ______________
19. When you enter a bank, do you talk to anyone or are you usually very quiet, as in a library? __________ If so, why? ______________

This section of your Personality Profile was developed to give you a deeper insight into how you perceive money in our society and how you perceive your own attitudes toward money.

Once again, there are no "right" or "wrong" answers to these questions. They should stimulate you to ask yourself more questions about how you can increase your skills as a money manager.

In those areas where you feel you are lacking in knowledge or understanding, you may want to start up your own reading program, take a night course, or consider hiring a specialist.

If you feel your own attitudes toward money may be getting in your way, you may wish to explore changing these attitudes.

Keep asking yourself questions like: Why do I think this? Where did I learn this? Should I change my thinking about this?

If, for example, you discover that you are a little afraid

of walking into a bank or talking to a lending officer about a loan, try to determine why this is so. See if you can come up with ways to change this attitude. Perhaps a visit to your bank would help. Practice applying for a small loan you really don't need. Take it out, put it in your savings account and pay it off after a few months just to give yourself this kind of experience. Use your imagination.

LESSON 3

DEVELOPING THE MILLIONAIRE'S ATTITUDE

Life is short. The sooner a man begins to enjoy his wealth the better.

—Samuel Johnson

Money has become much less important in our highly technical society. This has happened because high technology enables all but the poorest of us to share the same benefits. Wealthy and poor watch the same TV shows, ride the same freeways, shop in stores selling the same foods, eat in the same restaurants, see the same plays, symphonies and operas . . . in other words, *benefit* from our mobility and productivity.

What would you think of a person who was worth ten million dollars and complained he was poor? You would probably have very little sympathy for such a person, and yet millions of Americans act this way because they neither see the wealth around them nor do they appreciate its value.

When wealth was primarily valued in land ownership,

before our highly technological society, only the wealthy could afford luxuries. But today, these luxuries are within reach of us all. Products from around the world line the shelves of our stores. Parks provide the most elegant settings. Libraries provide limitless books, magazines, films, and other materials.

In other words, except for the abject poor, we all live like millionaires in our society. But so few of us adopt this attitude toward life. Many of us throw away a lifetime of opportunities because we "feel poor."

It is vital that each of us consider developing this "millionaire's attitude." This attitude can help free us from insecurity and inferiority about money. This attitude allows us to look through money to the opportunities we all have available to us.

You begin to manage your money successfully only after you defuse it of its power over you and remove the emotional chains it may wrap around you. If you look out at life through an attitude of poverty and low self-esteem, you will never be able to take control of your money. Money will always push you around. Money will force you to live your life on its terms. Money will make you a prisoner of this poverty attitude.

It will not be someone else who is restricting your potential. Your own attitude will be keeping you from living life as a free person on your own terms.

Learning this millionaire's attitude is vital to your success as a money manager. In reality, this attitude is simply the healthy attitude you can have toward yourself as a unique, valuable individual with every right to pursue your own dreams and goals. This attitude gives you an enormous freedom from the kind of misunderstanding about money you may have been dealing with in your past. A neutral or secure attitude toward money tends to open up your options and give you the best possible opportunities for getting what you want out of your life. By learning this attitude, you can eliminate many of the problems which may have restricted your thinking and life-style up until now.

THE MILLIONAIRE STRATEGY

The first step to mastering the millionaire's attitude is to use your imagination. For the moment, suspend those thoughts, attitudes, patterns and emotions you have stored up relating to money. State them, and then put them on a shelf. Close the door. They are there, but don't focus on them.

Instead, neutralize your thinking process so that you are able to look at money in a new way. In Lesson 1, we covered the six principal money attitudes and how each determines the way you will approach money management.

KEY POINT

> The millionaire's attitude gives you the best possible chance for learning how to manage your money well.

It is important to remember that your attitudes can be quite different from the reality of your life. You may be dead broke and that's a reality, but in spirit you may be brimming over with optimism, joy, and energy. The reality of your life may result from many outside factors, none of which you can control. Your attitudes, however, reflect the ways in which you evaluate what is happening.

There is the story of two millionaires who lost everything in the 1929 stock market crash. One leaped out of his office window, the other left for six months to fish in Canada.

Both expressed an attitude toward what had happened to them. Each came up with a solution.

We recommend you use the millionaire's attitude to guide your activities when a money crisis comes into your life or when you begin to feel you are getting nowhere.

SEE YOURSELF FREE

If you were a millionaire, how would you act? What would you buy? How would you spend your time? Imagine for a moment that you *are* a millionaire with more money than you can possibly spend. If this were true, what would you be doing with your life? How would you change it?

If money were not a problem, what would you be doing? Most of us get stuck in a "which-comes-first-the-chicken-or-the-egg?" attitude. We say we would like to do something but can't because we don't have enough money. We go round and round in circles, denying ourselves the pleasures and opportunities which are already coming our way.

By accepting the reality of your life and valuing what it is you have right now, you can automatically set yourself free of the chains which bind those who refuse to accept reality and who are always escaping from it or suffering because of it.

The principal point here is for you to consider thinking and acting as if you were a millionaire, as if money were no longer a problem in your life. Just as the millionaire values the power and freedom which come from controlling millions of dollars, you can value the power which comes from understanding the wealth you have right now in your life and enjoying it. Though you may not have millions of dollars, you can use the same attitudes that vast amounts of money often bring.

KEY POINT

> You don't have to become a millionaire to benefit from the millionaire's attitude. Whatever your situation right now, you can decide to live your life with the same peace of mind that often comes with wealth.

EVERYONE IS A MILLIONAIRE

There is an unusual thing that often happens with people. People value what they don't have *more* than what they do have!

For this reason, a person with a high school diploma often goes through life placing much more importance on a college diploma than someone who graduated from college does. A person who feels too tall values being short. A short person wants to be tall. People who can sing wish they could act and actors take singing lessons.

Every time we envy someone else or become depressed because we haven't got something someone else has, WE MOVE THE CENTER OF POWER AWAY FROM OUR OWN STRENGTHS.

This can result in our own personal weakness and a feeling of insecurity. Before you can ever hope to become a successful money manager, you've got to change your principal attitudes so that you value where you are right now and use your strengths to reach your maximum potential.

All of us are millionaires in the sense that we have talents, strengths and abilities. More than that, we have life. (This is not meant to be inspirational; it is *practical!*)

If a person cannot value what he or she already has, how can he or she hope to benefit from becoming a millionaire?

More money does not automatically bring security or increased happiness. To the contrary, more money can bring stress and insecurity if a person hasn't prepared for this increased wealth.

Each of us goes through life learning a process which determines how we will feel, act, and react to the things that happen to us in life. It is this process that can bring us peace of mind, joy, strength, and energy, not money, power, or material goods.

The secret of the millionaire's attitude is in valuing *yourself.* You place no other man or woman above you. You stand on an equal level, face to face, with every other person in the world. You don't pretend to compete with them in their areas of personal strengths. You are the world's number one expert on yourself. You value and enjoy your own life because you are contributing to the best of your ability.

And by valuing yourself, your *self-value* will shine through. When you meet strangers, friends, and family you will carry a "presence" which will be powerful.

Once you have gained this insight into yourself and where you are in relation to other people, you can then begin to manage your money effectively, because *you* will be deciding what it is you want to do with it.

MONEY IS NOT IMPORTANT AFTER ALL

There is a point in people's lives when they realize they have acquired the amount of money they think they "need" to satisfy their particular self-image. In other words, a person feels that he or she has finally "got it made." Money over and above this amount can become unimportant to them.

For some people the amount of money they need to feel secure is $600 a month. For others, it is $1,500 a month.

The point is that everyone has an inner idea of how much money it takes to "fill the insecurity gap."

By using the millionaire's attitude you can eliminate the long struggle to reach whatever figure may be the security figure in your life and start out today being content and secure with whatever amount of money it is you already have.

In other words, you can save yourself a lot of grief by deciding you don't want to play the "money security game."

The moment you reprogram your attitudes toward life and aim your energy at getting the things you want out of life, you remove these limitations and open up doors of unlimited opportunity.

FORGET MONEY! Stop worrying about it. Don't complain because you don't have enough of it. Instead, enjoy what you've got and make plans to use the rest of your life getting the most out of whatever wealth you might acquire.

KEY POINT

> You have the *poverty attitude* when you value what other people have more than you value what you have.
>
> You have the *millionaire's attitude* when you value what you have more than you value what other people have.

ELIMINATE THE MANIPULATORS

You really begin to take control over your money when you no longer set your goals by what your family, your friends, your TV, or your local newspaper says—but by what it is *you* want.

If you cannot control the effect of "manipulators" in your life, you will never be able to resist spending your money to buy what they are selling. The millionaire does not rush out and buy everything someone else tells him or her to buy. That's one of the reasons a person becomes a millionaire.

Instead, the millionaire practices control over what he or she spends so that a productive balance between income and expenses is reached.

Ben Franklin said it a long time ago: "A happy person makes $100 a week and spends $99. An unhappy person makes $100 a week and spends $101."

You become a millionaire when you master this *process.*

KEY POINT

> You become a successful money manager when you are convinced you have sufficient self-control to be able to live within your income.

When you know you can resist all those people out there trying to get you to spend your money for their benefit, you can begin to spend your money your way. You control your expenses by controlling your *desires and needs.*

If you have determined that you need an expensive imported sports car, a large home in an exclusive neighborhood, membership in a country club, season tickets at the opera, a month's vacation in Europe, a vacation home in ski country, a private school for your three children, custom-made clothes, and your own private collection of modern art . . . you are creating a need for a lot of income to support your life-style. If you can afford it, great! If not, you're headed for trouble.

If you decide you need a Honda, a cottage to live in, public schools for your children, a camping vacation and you spend your time using public facilities—libraries, pools and parks, golf courses—and a wealth of other inexpensive means of entertaining and enriching your life . . . you are creating a need for a limited amount of income to support your life-style.

OPPORTUNITIES FOR EVERYONE

The richness of life does not depend on how much money you make. Love, friendship, excitement, service, health, joy, pleasure, and personal growth all operate outside the world of money.

You become a "millionaire" by learning how to seek out and enjoy the things you want in the environment in which you now live. You've moved the millionaire's *attitude* into the state of *being* a "millionaire." It is the personal growth you experience inside that brings psychological peace of mind and "wealth" into your life.

By starting now with what you've already got, and thanking your lucky stars you've got it, you will begin to learn the appreciation of wealth. With appreciation will come understanding and with understanding . . . freedom.

HEY . . . YOU SAID THIS WAS A PRACTICAL PROGRAM!

Right now, you may be saying, "OK, so I know all this. What's this got to do with money management? Where are the practical methods I can use to make more money? Let's get on with it!"

The point is that unless you gain an insight into what money really is, and who *you* really are, all those "practical methods" won't do you a bit of good.

If you are having money problems, if you never seem to be getting anywhere, and if you are bored with your life, your *attitude* toward life and your misunderstanding of what life is may be creating these problems.

Making more money won't solve your problems. More money may temporarily mask your problems and it may appear that you have solved them, but sooner or later new problems will crop up.

This program is designed to give you a real insight into how you can reprogram your life to make it pay off for you. That's why we are spending five lessons reviewing the psychological meaning of money as it influences your life.

Before you can ever hope to control money, you've got to reprogram thinking and behavior patterns you may have formed about money. Until you see how those attitudes are holding you back, you won't be motivated to change them. And if you don't formulate a plan to change them, you will be staying right where you are now.

SUMMARY

The poverty attitude says, "I can't do anything I really want to do because I don't have the money to do it."

The millionaire's attitude says, "There is no limit to what I can do if I am willing to pay the price and be realistic about what it is I want to do."

When you have mastered the millionaire's attitude you will seldom experience the negative emotions that come from having less money than someone else. You will value yourself and the gifts life has made available to you, and you won't continuously suffer from the mistakes you have made or the setbacks you have experienced. You will begin to build the rest of your life, one day at a time, from where you are right now. You will live your life secure in that you are no longer manipulated by what other people want you to do and be, but are directed by your own inner desires.

Having reached this level of understanding about money, you are now ready to develop your own personal money management strategy.

Turn now to Section 3 of the Personality Profile and take no more than ten minutes to complete it. In each column, check the answer that most applies to the way you think right now. After you have completed this section, add up the number of checks in the right-hand column and then add up the checks in the left-hand column. Answers in the right-hand column indicate that you are not yet practicing the millionaire's attitude. Answers in the left-hand column indicate that you are practicing the millionaire's attitude. Your score should give you a good idea of how much reprogramming you may need to change your attitude in the future.

DO NOT GO ON TO LESSON 4 UNTIL TOMORROW.

PERSONALITY PROFILE

SECTION 3
DEVELOPING THE MILLIONAIRE'S ATTITUDE

1. How do you feel about yourself?
   - __I enjoy life and value what I have.
   - __Money is just one of many resources I use.
   - __I am in control of myself.
   - __There are many things I enjoy doing.
   - __Life is a wonderful gift.
   - __Excitement comes from inner peace of mind.
   - __There are many things I enjoy which don't cost money.
   - __I determine where my life is going.
   - __I envy people with more money.
   - __Without a lot of money, life is dull and frustrating.
   - __I need more money to be happy.
   - __It takes money to have friends and fun.
   - __Some people get all the breaks.
   - __Rich people have all the fun.
   - __I escape from my life because I can't afford to do the things I want to do.
   - __If it weren't for my family, I could get ahead of things.

__There are unlimited opportunities for me.

__When I need advice, I seek it from qualified specialists.

__I enjoy my work and believe it to be worthwhile.

__Life is a gift.

__I never got any breaks. I never had any luck with money.

__The system is against the common wage earner. The big shots have all the power.

__I would like to switch jobs but I'm too old.

__Life is a prison.

2. How do you perceive money? What does money mean to you?

__Money is useful, a resource.

__By managing it well, I use it to achieve my personal objectives.

__Money is a convenience I use to exchange skills for income and things I buy.

__When I take a financial loss I forget about it.

__I concentrate on my own skills and self-development.

__I have a plan for managing my money.

__Lack of money never keeps me from enjoying myself.

__Money is vital to survival.

__Money makes the world go round. I never have enough of it to enjoy the things I want to do.

__Money is power. It can buy everything.

__I can't stand to lose money.

__I seek ways to get rich, to have more money to spend.

__I'm looking for the secret way to get rich.

__At the end of the month, I'm bored to death because there is nothing interesting to do.

__I live within my means.	__I'm always in debt.
__I would rather have my health than money any day.	__Nothing is more important than having money.
__I accept what life brings me and make the most of it.	__If only I had more money, my life would be wonderful.
TOTAL	TOTAL

In each case where you have marked a check in the right-hand column, you have red-flagged an area in which your attitudes may be standing in your way.

Since successful money management results from mastering a process, the more you can reprogram your attitudes to parallel reality, the better chances you will have to succeed as a money manager.

In each case where you have checked a right-hand column, try to see if you can determine why you have this attitude. Don't worry about this now. In the reprogramming lesson you will learn a 7-step method you can use to change attitudes like this.

LESSON 4

MASTERING THE BASICS OF SUCCESSFUL MONEY MANAGEMENT

> **The darkest hour in any man's life is when he sits down to plan how to get money without earning it.**
>
> **—Horace Greeley**

In the first three lessons, we reviewed how money works and what attitudes you can have which will influence the amount of money you will probably end up managing. Once you have determined the money attitudes you want to have, you can then begin to develop strategies and plans for achieving your financial objectives.

In this lesson we are going to outline a 10-step, cash flow management system you can use to gain control over your cash flow.

Cash flow is a term we use to measure the way cash or money flows through your account on a daily, weekly, or monthly basis. Each month you will receive so much income. During the month you will spend so much of it on food, rent, entertainment, paying bills, etc.

If at the end of the month you have spent more than you have earned, you are in trouble unless you reverse this trend, because in order to balance your expenses with your income, you will have to use some of your capital.

So your primary income money management goal is to maintain your cash flow so that you have a little money left over each month to add to your capital account.

The basic techniques we will cover in this lesson apply to almost everyone who manages his or her own money. These techniques are the fundamental steps to successful money management.

Read through these 10 steps and be sure you understand each one. You will want to come back and review these 10 steps over and over until you use them automatically. Once you have mastered these basic principles, you will then be ready to explore borrowing, credit, investments, building an estate, and other processes relating to money that become important ONLY AFTER YOU HAVE MASTERED THESE 10 BASIC CASH FLOW MANAGEMENT STEPS!

If you want to enjoy your money, even if it is a monthly welfare check, you've got to be in control of it. You've got to know *you* are deciding how it will be spent. You've got to be confident you are playing your game with your money. Once you know this, you can begin to explore new opportunities for increasing your income.

Begin following this 10-step cash flow management system today and experience the rewards that come from knowing that, finally, you are in control of what is happening to you financially.

THE 10-STEP CASH FLOW MANAGEMENT SYSTEM

STEP 1: BUY A POCKET CALCULATOR

Before the pocket calculator, the excuse "I can't add or subtract" had some merit. There are those of us (like myself) who simply aren't skilled in adding and subtracting numbers. But the pocket calculator has changed all that. It makes working with numbers fun—like playing pinball. You can buy one for less than $15 and it will pay enormous dividends.

STEP 2: OPEN TWO FAMILY SAVINGS ACCOUNTS. OPEN ONE CHECKING ACCOUNT FOR EACH CHILD OVER FOURTEEN WHO HAS DEMONSTRATED AN ABILITY TO USE IT PROPERLY.

More money trouble comes from two people trying to use the same checking account and keep it in balance than practically any other single cause. The arguments husbands and wives have had over bouncing checks and unbalanced checking accounts would stretch from here to the moon. Let each member of your family be responsible for managing his or her own checking account.

Your *children* should have their own checking and savings accounts too. You are preparing them to survive in the adult world. What better way than to give them the opportunity of managing their own money? They'll love you for it. They will gain confidence. And it will give them an excellent start toward effective money management.

For younger children, practice taking time to sit down with them and show them how your checking account works. Let them help you pay bills, write out checks, etc., until they have a thorough understanding of how a checking account works. When you feel they have gained sufficient confidence, open up a checking account for them. Use this whenever you buy school clothes, give them money for Christmas presents, etc.

The reason you should open two savings accounts is that you are going to start putting away money for future purchases instead of using credit cards (the worst thing that has happened to the average wage earner since the 1929 depression). You are going to want to separate real savings (or your increase in capital) from savings put away to be spent within the next year for such things as vacations and taxes.

There is no worse way to start a vacation than to be angry when you go to the bank to draw out money from your savings account to buy traveler's checks. So don't look at it as money saved. Look at it as money put away (temporarily) to be spent later on.

STEP 3: KEEP CLEAR, ACCURATE RECORDS

All of us today are required to keep accurate records for tax purposes. By paying your bills by check, you automatically end up with a running record of your expenses. At the end of the year you can use this record to prepare your taxes. You can also use this running record to see how you are doing each month, each week, or each day if you want to.

Accurate record-keeping is essential to successful money management. There is simply no way you can control your money without clear, precise, accurate records.

If you would rather keep your receipts at the bottom of your purse or in the glove compartment of your car, if you don't want to take time to write checks . . . forget becoming a successful money manager. MONEY MANAGEMENT BEGINS AND ENDS WITH KEEPING CLEAR, AC-

CURATE RECORDS. If you simply won't keep the records yourself, PAY someone else to do it for you. But be sure it's done.

STEP 4: DON'T PREPARE YOUR OWN TAX RETURNS

If you really want to increase your capital, you are going to have to learn to work with other people to do so—with bankers, attorneys, CPAs, brokers, and so on. Even if you are now living on a fixed income, take your taxes to a professional and let him or her prepare them!

Professional tax preparation is the best buy you can make today. Taxes are too complicated to spend your time trying to make the extra buck doing your own. Get in the habit of paying someone else to get the job done for you. This trains you to work with other professional financial people and gives you the experience you will need as you begin to invest your surplus capital.

Don't cheat on your taxes! Go the extra mile to make sure you are honestly declaring only legitimate deductions and expenses. It's simply not worth it to cheat a little on your tax payments. However, do everything you can to take every legitimate deduction you are allowed. Structure your investments to give you the best tax breaks possible, but don't be dishonest.

It is in your best interest to do this. As you accumulate more capital, you increase the likelihood that you will be audited. Your best protection against an adverse audit is to be honest. This way, you can look the auditor in the face, *knowing* that you have done everything you can to pay your fair share of taxes.

If you have paid someone else to do your taxes, they will go with you to the audit. This alone is worth the small fee you pay them to do your taxes.

Get in the habit of being an honest partner with the government and you will be able to prosper without the nagging fear that someday you will be found out.

STEP 5: PAY EVERYTHING BY CHECK

Your checkbook is your best record. By using it to pay as many of your bills as is convenient, you have an automatic record of where your money is going. Get in the habit of writing a check for each of your bills and purchases over $5 or $10. A check takes only a minute or two to write out and gives you a valuable record of your expenses each month.

Obviously, you will not want to write a check for everything you buy. It is a good idea to set up a monthly cash fund to handle miscellaneous expenses each day. You can also use credit cards and charge accounts to record your purchases as long as you make sure to pay off the balances on a monthly basis so that you do not pay 18% or more interest on your own money. In other words, you want to have some freedom to spend your money without always worrying about every dollar, but at the same time you want to keep a current record of your expenses so that you can see where you are heading financially while at the same time developing an accurate base for determining your taxes each year.

Get in the habit of paying your bills with checks and you will have an excellent money management technique at your disposal.

STEP 6: PAY YOURSELF FIRST

Pay yourself first! Think about this for a moment. This is one of the most important things you will read in this money management program. The only way you will successfully accumulate increasing amounts of capital is to PAY YOURSELF FIRST.

If you are like most of us, you have been working all your life paying everyone as best you can—on time or close to it. You worry about paying the dentist, the doctor, the mortgage, the car payment, the insurance policy, and so on.

What about yourself? You are doing the working. You are spending your life earning this money. Why put yourself at the end of the line? You deserve to be paid for your labor. You are entitled to be paid. You are worthy of being paid.

So start out right now and put yourself at the head of the list. Each month, pay yourself first. When the old paycheck comes in, make sure the first check of the month is written out to yourself.

How much you pay yourself is up to you. It depends on how much you believe your labor is worth vis-à-vis the labor of all those other people you are paying. But whatever the amount, get into the habit of paying yourself *something.* Make out a check to yourself and then deposit it in your permanent savings account. Even if you are in the bank with your savings book, your checkbook and your paycheck, don't just credit funds into the savings account. Put all the money into your checking account and then write a check to yourself and deposit it in your savings account.

Don't spend capital! Once you have paid yourself, you transform that money from income into capital. Use your capital only to invest to earn more money for you. Don't spend your capital on anything that won't earn income for you. It is by building up your capital base that you are going to finally get *free* of having to work to earn money.

Your objective is to build your capital account to the point where the income it earns pays all your monthly expenses. Once this happens, you are then free to spend your life doing whatever it is you want to do, even if this means going right on doing what you are doing now.

PAY YOURSELF FIRST. PAY YOURSELF FIRST. PAY YOURSELF FIRST. Repeat this over and over again until you begin to PAY YOURSELF FIRST each month on a regular basis.

WHAT IS CAPITAL?

If you do not understand what capital is, there is very little chance you will ever become a successful money manager. Money management begins with capital and the primary objective of money management is to build up your capital.

Capital is money you have left over at the end of the year after you have paid your taxes and your current liabilities (bills). It is *money you have already paid taxes on.* This is extremely important, because it is worth much more to you than ordinary income. Why?

Suppose you are paying a 40% tax on your income each year. For every dollar you earn, you pay out $.40 in taxes. You also have to use income to pay your bills, buy food, etc. However, once you transform an income dollar into capital it goes to work for you. When you invest capital, it earns income for you.

Every time you spend a dollar of your capital, you are paying a double penalty, because you are losing its investment potential and replacing it with an income dollar on which you have to pay taxes all over again.

The most important objective of money management is to continue to transform money into capital during your life so that as you grow older, your capital earns you money.

People who have accumulated enough capital to earn themselves an income equal to their needs experience financial security. As you develop your own personal money plan, you should always be working to increase your capital

. . . spending it only as a last resort in the event of a serious emergency.

STEP 7: PAY YOUR FIXED EXPENSES

Write out checks each month for all your recurring monthly expenses—your mortgage payment, your car payment, etc. If you have unpaid bills on hand, which you are paying off on a monthly basis, write checks for these also.

Even though the actual payment may not be due until the end of the month, write out the check anyway and deduct it from your checking account balance. If you are paid every two weeks, start off each month with the amount you will be paid for the whole month. Then write these checks. If you need to wait until your second paycheck to cover these checks, then place them in an envelope and wait until after you have made your second deposit to mail them out.

KEY POINT

> Your objective is to deduct from your monthly income all the *known* monthly expenses you will have during the month. This frees your energy to concentrate on other things and prevents you from worrying about not being able to pay your important bills each month. You will know on the first of the month how much money you are going to have left over to spend. In other words, you are now managing your money; your money isn't managing you.

STEP 8: BUY YOUR NECESSITY ITEMS

You should also be able to predict approximately how much you will need to spend for groceries, gas, utilities, phone bills, etc. All of these are expenses you *know* you will have before the end of the month.

Estimate how much this will come to and either transfer it to your spouse's account for his or her use if he or she is taking care of the daily living budget or, if you are single, leave it in your checking account.

It is vital that you keep track of your daily living expenses, because it is here that most of us lose a lot of our money. We get nickled and dimed out of our hard-earned cash. It just seems to disappear.

STEP 9: PUT AWAY YOUR EMERGENCY MONEY

Why is it we are always so surprised when we discover that the old 1967 Volkswagen needs a new engine at a cost of $650? How come we are surprised when the dishwasher we got fifteen years ago finally breaks down?

Emergencies come . . . to everyone. You can't anticipate all of them but you can *protect* yourself against most of them. So estimate what you think could be some of the emergencies that might come up over the next twelve months and begin depositing money each month into your savings account so that when an emergency happens, you aren't behind.

STEP 10: USE WHAT'S LEFT OVER FOR ENTERTAINMENT

On the first of the month, after you have made all of the above deductions, if you are managing your money successfully and have not incurred expenses or debts which have totally depleted your money supply or income, you will usually have some money left over. Use this money any way you like. It's yours. You deserve it. Have fun. It's your reward for becoming a successful money manager.

KEY POINT

If you are now in a position where your debts and current expenses so far exceed your income that no matter how well you manage your money, you will not have any left over for entertaining yourself or your family . . . it is STILL A GOOD IDEA TO BUDGET SOME MONEY TO BE USED IN THIS WAY.

It may not be much, but the boost in morale you and your family will get by doing this will be far more important than the few extra dollars you pay to one creditor or another. This in itself can be an incentive for you to begin to really take control over your money so that you increase this entertainment budget (your reward) even more as you develop improved money management skills.

SUMMARY

Let's review the checking and savings accounts a family of three should have. Assume that both husband and wife are working full time and they have a fourteen-year-old daughter.

1. CHECKING ACCOUNT A:

This account is the husband's or wife's personal checking account into which all his or her monthly income is credited. From it, the wage earner pays himself or herself *first* with the first check of each month. Then he or she pays whatever fixed expenses are assigned to him or her and then contributes whatever he or she has agreed to contribute to the monthly living expenses account and the emergency account. The money that is left over after all these deductions have been made is the entertainment money, or money which can be spent in whatever way the person wants.

2. CHECKING ACCOUNT B:

This account is used by the other spouse in the same way.

3. CHECKING ACCOUNT C:

This is the account you will be setting up for the fourteen-year-old daughter. You will want to use your judgment as to whether you actually set up an account in her name or merely work with her to show her how your checking account works. A lot will depend upon her maturity and the amount of money she will be spending over a year's time.

The important point is to show her how to use a checking account. The sooner she understands how it works, the better chance she has of becoming a successful money manager herself. Since a teen-ager cannot go around using checks to pay for things (at the school cafeteria, movies, etc.), you should set up a cash account for her to use for these expenses. Encourage her to keep a daily record of how much she spends and why she spends it. This should be her own confidential and personal record, not something you use to check up on her purchases.

This eliminates her dependence for spending money and upgrades an allowance into an adult relationship within the family. After all, she is earning her share of the income just as much as her parents are.

Now when the end of the month rolls around and she is broke, she can see how this happened.

4. SAVINGS ACCOUNT A:

This joint savings account should be used for your capital funds—funds that are put away to invest, not to spend on vacations, new TV sets, etc. It is this account that is the seed which will grow into wealth. Nurture it, protect it, profit from it.

KEY POINT

> Your rule for withdrawing money from this account should be: "I only spend money from this account to invest in something that is going to earn me more money."

5. SAVINGS ACCOUNT B:

This joint savings account is to be used for planned expenses that are sure to come up during the year: vacations, emergencies, long term expenses (such as braces for the fourteen-year-old daughter), college tuition, etc.

KEY POINT

> Your rule for withdrawing money from this account is: "I only withdraw money from this account for things I have planned ahead for, such as emergencies and non-income earning purchases (e.g., a TV set, a new car, a stereo)."

6. SAVINGS ACCOUNT C:

This is the fourteen-year-old daughter's savings account into which she puts money but does not withdraw.

YOU'VE GOT TO BE KIDDING?

Six checking and savings accounts for three people? What is this? I'm just making the banks rich, huh?

No, you are starting out to become a successful money manager. Wealthy individuals with money scattered around in different investments keep accurate books for each separate account. You can eliminate the charges on these checking accounts by maintaining a minimum balance. Some banks offer free checking accounts.

Setting up your personal financial system like this will pay enormous dividends to you and your family not only in terms of financial rewards, but also in terms of family harmony. You will all be working together to manage your family money. You will share with one another the responsibilities and the realities of surviving on your own terms.

WHAT TO DO WITH GIFTS AND LARGE SUMS OF UNEXPECTED MONEY

Money you inherit or money that comes in at Christmas or on a birthday can be handled in any way you like. How you use it will depend on your own situation, the amount of money which comes in, your present and future needs, etc.

A large inheritance can substantially improve your capital position. It could become the down payment on the house you always wanted, money to support a new career, etc. Smaller sums, especially money which children often receive, can add up to quite a sum over the years if they are treated as capital and placed in the permanent savings account.

The important thing to watch out for is that this sudden increase in extra money does not "go to your head" and totally throw off your short- and long-range money management strategy. Sudden windfalls of large sums of money can cause difficult personal problems if they are not handled intelligently. You will want to use your best judgment in deciding how much of this money to use as income (for paying bills, buying luxury items, etc.) and how much of it to use as capital (for your savings account or some other investment). It is always a good idea to put at least part of this money into your capital account since it automatically increases the amount of capital you have.

KEY POINT

Once you have mastered the essentials of cash flow control, you have gone most of the way toward becoming a successful money manager. This skill is the key to making your financial plans work.

In the next five lessons, we are going to cover in detail the techniques you can use to develop your own personal money strategy and money plans. The objective of managing your money is to develop skills which will enable you to control the flow of money in *your* direction. By practicing these ten money management techniques, you and your family can develop this control.

Turn now to Section 4 of your Personality Profile and complete it. The objective of this section is to give you an idea of how well you are now controlling your cash flow.

DO NOT GO ON TO LESSON 5 UNTIL TOMORROW.

PERSONALITY PROFILE

SECTION 4
MASTERING THE BASICS OF SUCCESSFUL MONEY MANAGEMENT

1. Are all your important financial documents (life insurance policy, mortgage, stocks, bonds, savings passbook, etc.) in one place where every adult member of the family has access in case of emergency? ______
2. If you are married does your spouse share with you your financial objectives and management on a regular basis? If not, why not? ______
3. Do your children share in the family financial affairs and have their own money to manage? ______
4. Do you or any other member of your family continually shop and buy things on an impulse basis? ______
5. Do you or any other member of your family support a money-draining habit (for example, excessive drinking, smoking, gambling)? ______
6. Does each member of your family over fourteen have a personal checking account? ______
7. Do you keep clear, accurate records of your expenses? ______
8. Do you prepare your own tax returns? ______
   If so, why? ______
9. Do you pay for everything by check? ______
   If you use a credit card to pay for things, do you keep

a running balance on which you pay monthly interest? If so, why? ______

10. Do you pay yourself first each month? ______ If not, why not? ______
11. Do you deduct your fixed expenses (mortgage payment, car payment, etc.) at the beginning of the month? ______
12. Do you have a fixed budget for necessity items (food, clothing, household goods, etc.)? ______
13. Do you put away money for emergencies each month? ______
14. If you run out of money at the end of the month do you stop spending money on entertainment and luxuries?
15. Is your family able to live within the budgets you set each month? ______ If not, why not? ______
16. Can you think of at least three ways you and your family can better control your cash flow?
    a. ______
    b. ______
    c. ______

HOW TO EVALUATE YOUR PERSONALITY PROFILE

These questions are designed to start you thinking about the practical way you are now controlling your cash flow. Hopefully, this section of your Personality Profile may have red-flagged some areas in which money is being drained away from your supply each month. If so, you will want to begin to develop plans for changing your attitudes and life-style so that you "fix the leak" and increase the available money you have on hand.

Every time you can reduce the amount of income you spend while maintaining or increasing your life-style, you are moving closer to being able to take total control over your money.

LESSON 5

SELECTING YOUR OWN MONEY MANAGEMENT STRATEGY

> **That man is the richest whose pleasures are the cheapest.**
>
> **—Thoreau**

The next step to successful money management is to determine precisely what kind of a life you want to live from now on and whether it is realistic to expect you will achieve it. What is it you want from life? What is it you are willing to pay? Do you want to be a doctor, a professional tennis player, a carpenter, potter, or clerk?

By asking yourself a number of important personal questions, you will complete your own personal financial profile, which will give you, in writing, a road map to the future you want for yourself. You will be able to measure how close or far you are from being able to live this lifestyle.

You will now have a starting place and a destination, and you will be able to determine what it will cost you to get there. And since you now have a destination, you will be going someplace.

Until you have written down this "life plan," you have not yet created the essential means to begin your journey. Everything begins to happen *your* way after you have stepped forward toward an objective. Your trip can't begin until you have identified your objective.

If you choose to drift through life, that's OK if that's what you really want to do. But then don't complain when you aren't getting the breaks or when life isn't treating you fairly.

YOU CAN DO ANYTHING YOU BELIEVE YOU CAN DO

Not true! There are a lot of these "you can do anything" books out on the market today . . . and they are dangerous. There are hundreds of things you cannot do and never will be able to do (or even if you could do them, the effort wouldn't be worth it). For starters, try to get the U.S. Congress to cut back its salaries, or try to sell your own prescription drugs in the United States without FDA approval.

The point here is that though there *are* many, many things each of us can do, there are only a limited amount of things we can do successfully in our lifetime. Persistence is great. Dedication is wonderful. But spending your life chasing an impossible dream is a poor way to enjoy the prosperity that surrounds us.

The best approach is to seek out and find things that really turn you on. Find things you can do and like to do, and then apply your energies to these areas of your life. Your primary objective in writing up your own money management strategy is to select objectives that you can achieve, and then align these objectives to your personal financial situation.

You now know that money isn't a force you work against, something out there over which you have no control. To the contrary, it is a resource over which you have *enormous* control. No matter how little or how much money you have right now, you can begin to practice sound, effective money management techniques which will help to automatically develop and increase the amount you have available.

You have seen that most people are held back not because they lack money or were born poor, but because their own poverty attitudes, fears, insecurities, and failure behavior patterns have restricted their activities.

Understanding this, you can see that the key technique for becoming a successful money manager is to hammer out your own personal life-style strategy, and then align it to your financial situation to come up with a feasible plan for the future.

In this lesson you will learn how to develop that strategy for getting what *you* want (not what your husband or wife, your parents, children, or friends want out of your life).

GETTING DOWN TO BASICS

Each of us is totally unique in our money situation. No two people have exactly the same amount of money, money objectives, or money problems. Husbands and wives have different money considerations even though they share the same money supply.

There are different levels of money. As we have seen, money works for you when you have larger amounts of it. It can work against you when you don't. The extra amount of money you have over your monthly expenses is called capital. Capital is money you can use to invest. When you invest money you buy something. That something may be real (a house, a painting, a farm, an office building), or it may be symbolic (a share of stock, a savings account, and so on).

Your ability to survive depends upon being able to earn enough money each month to pay your bills. The monthly income you have is called cash flow. Cash flow is the amount of money coming into your account and the money going out of your account. When you spend more than you earn, you have a negative cash flow. When you spend less than you earn, you have a positive cash flow.

It is important that you look at your cash flow situation from both a short- and a long-range point of view. Many people end up broke later on, because they didn't plan for the time when their earnings would be reduced. Your personal money management plan depends upon your specific goals. If you really want to live on social security when you're old, fine. Don't plan ahead. Spend more of your income now and enjoy it. But don't complain if you retire to live in semipoverty. You did it to yourself.

MONEY MANAGEMENT—WHAT IT'S ALL ABOUT

Once you decide you want to become a successful money manager, you are going to be interested in controlling six important areas in your financial life:

1. Your money attitudes
2. Your income
3. Your expenses
4. Your debt level

5. Your assets (investments, things you can sell)
6. Your rewards

By controlling these areas effectively, you become *aware* of what you are doing; you come to recognize the money traps and opportunities around you. The successful money manager avoids as many of these money traps as possible and takes advantage of as many opportunities as he or she can.

In the beginning you may find you have to put in more time and effort to get things together and take control over these six important areas in your financial life, but after a while things begin to move forward smoothly and automatically so that you can spend less time monitoring your progress and devote more time to other areas of your life.

1. YOUR MONEY ATTITUDES

We have already covered the importance of developing the major money attitude you will need to achieve the financial goals you decide to set for yourself. (You will learn how to reprogram changes in your thinking and attitude patterns in the next lesson.)

Along with your major attitudes, you are going to want to develop the concerns, skills, interests, and thinking patterns that successful, professional money managers pay attention to.

Basically, as a successful money manager, you want to be sure you are aware of the economic conditions that determine what will happen over the coming years (e.g., inflation, tight money markets, high interest rates). You want to be sure your capital is wisely invested in the best possible opportunities for *you.*

As a successful money manager, you also want to be sure that you have sufficient control over income and outgo (cash flow) of whatever money you have to manage. Without this control, the mechanics of money management won't produce the results you are looking for. (It's like an ocean liner that springs a big leak. Unless the leak is controlled and contained, the ship will sink and never get to its destination.)

So there are two basics—financial awareness and financial control—that you will use (along with risk-taking, loss-cutting, and other skills) to set and reach your financial goals.

KEY POINT

> The primary money management objective is to keep income each month higher than expenses.

If this is the only money management technique you ever use, it can work wonders for your life. As long as you are generating a little surplus money each month, you are increasing your capital account (i.e., money you don't need to spend and can therefore use to invest in opportunities which will earn you additional money).

Unfortunately, few of us can expect to be able to maintain or increase our personal earning power throughout our lives. There is in fact a classic earnings pattern through which most of us go:

Age	Earning Power
0–18 years	Negative. Someone else is supporting us. We are learning the skills which we will sell.
19–65	Positive. Our working years. We generally

	increase our earning power through seniority, etc. However, the years from 45 to 65 can be difficult if we lose our job. Sometimes we have to switch careers and work for less than we were making.
65–up	Negative. Our *personal* earning power usually goes down. We are retired. Age and illness can cut down our capacity to earn money.*

Usually, the only thing that can reverse the natural trend of decreased earning power when we are older is our ability to accumulate capital. In other words, if we are successful money managers during our working years, we can build up an estate which pays us income in our older years.

Being a successful money manager means that you strike a balance between your money needs right now and what you anticipate your needs will be later in life.

So you have two questions to ask yourself every day:

1. Am I living within my income right now?
2. Am I managing my income so I will have a surplus when I retire?

The beginning of money management is being able to generate income. Without a source of income, there will be no money to manage.

2. YOUR INCOME

Income can come from many sources. It can come from your job, from interest on your savings, from your spouse's job, from the rental of your house, from selling something

*Here we are talking about "wages" for personal labor, not "income" from investments.

you make, from lending money to other people, from insurance, and so on.

KEY POINT

> If you are in a situation where you cannot earn income you don't have a money management problem, you have a *survival* problem. You must either develop the skills to start earning income or become either a ward of the state or dependent on someone else who can earn income—a spouse, a son, a daughter.

Once you have identified your source of income, you can then project how much money you will be earning this month, next month, and so on.

This projection will give you an idea of your spending power. If you are sixty-four years old and know you will be retiring in six months, chances are it isn't the time to rush out and buy a big house that will triple your monthly mortgage payments.

If you are a union member, a civil servant, or a salaried employee, you can generally project the level of income you can count on during your working years.

The same is true with other professions: Each will have its own mix of security and income level.

A very important step to managing your money successfully is to be absolutely honest with yourself about how much your income really is. This means how much spendable income you will have after deducting taxes and other required payments. You've got to *know* this figure, because it gives you your money management starting place. So you will come up with a figure:

I make $550 a month, spendable take-home pay.
I make $1,100 a month, spendable take-home pay.
I make $25,000 a month, spendable take-home pay.

KEY POINT

Successful money management is learning to keep your expenses below your income.

3. YOUR EXPENSES

Your third important step is to determine your expenses. Unless you know your *real* expenses each month, you cannot determine whether you are coming out ahead or behind in your campaign to keep your expenses below your income.

So you have to take time to add up all your monthly expenses. Make sure you include them all. This means anticipating expenses that may come only every three months or twice a year or once a year—expenses such as property taxes, car insurance, and dentist's bills.

Average these expenses out over the year by dividing the annual amount by twelve.

What you are doing is trying to *predict* what your expenses will be over the coming months. Don't try to be 100% accurate; leave a little leeway for unexpected expenses or things you want to buy on impulse. Primarily, your objective is to pin down what income you will need to cover these expenses. So you will come up with a figure:

I spend $570 a month.
I spend $900 a month.
I spend $29,000 a month.

You must know these two key figures in order to be able to manage your money. Managing money is the skill of controlling income and expenses so that you come out ahead and not behind. Since most of us do not have the opportunity to control our income at will (i.e., to dramatically increase it any time we want to), it follows that *the most control we have over our cash flow is our control over our expenses.*

KEY POINT

> In the beginning, and until you get to the point where you have accumulated sufficient capital to invest, your primary money management skills are going to be used in controlling your *expenses,* not your income.

Until you have learned to control your expenses, you cannot expect to manage your money so that you begin to save money or accumulate capital. So forget the get-rich-quick and the how-to-make-a-million-dollars-overnight books for now. Even if you were lucky and did suddenly make a lot of money fast, unless you have learned the art of controlling your expenses, it won't be long before you are in a sea of debt and complicated tax problems.

WHO IS THE BEST MONEY MANAGER?

Which of these people is managing their money better?

INCOME	EXPENSES
$ 550	$ 570
$ 1,100	$ 900
$25,000	$29,000

Only one of these three people is managing their money successfully:

INCOME	EXPENSES	SURPLUS/LOSS
$ 550	$ 570	−$ 20
$ 1,100	$ 900	+$ 200
$25,000	$29,000	−$4,000

How many times have you said, "If only I were making $25,000 a year, I'd have it made!"?

Now this person who is making $25,000 a month is going into debt at the rate of $4,000 a month; he or she is *losing* $48,000 a year. The person making $550 a month is going into debt at the rate of $20 a month or $240 a year. The person making $1,100 a month is gaining $200 a month or $2,400 a year.

At this rate, in ten years:

INCOME	SURPLUS/LOSS
$ 550 will have lost	−$ 2,400
$ 1,100 will have gained	+$ 24,000
$25,000 will have lost	−$480,000

When you have learned how to control your income and your expenses so that you are able to increase your savings on a regular basis, you have mastered the most important skill of a successful money manager.

Your next step is to understand how to use credit. Until you are able to control your debt level, you may find that years of effective control of your income and expenses are ruined by excessive debt. This can happen suddenly and lead to painful and discouraging readjustments in your life-style and eventually, in many cases, bankruptcy.

4. YOUR DEBT LEVEL

Debt is simply a way of measuring how much you owe someone else. Usually, debt is acquired through borrowing money on credit. When you borrow small amounts, you probably won't have to worry about securing the money you borrow with collateral. Collateral is something valuable that you give the lender rights to so that he or she can sell it to recover his or her money should you not repay it.

Large amounts of borrowed money usually require some kind of collateral (your home, your car, your savings passbook, etc.).

The debt level you select will depend upon your major financial strategy. If, for example, you decide to teach English in a high school as a career, you will probably keep your debt level relatively low, with your house and your car representing your biggest debts. However, if you decide to start your own chain of restaurants, you may end up with a debt level of millions of dollars.

We will cover the subject of credit and debt in detail in Lesson 8. The important thing to remember here is that you are going to want to keep a tight control over your debt level; use credit only to advance your financial objectives and not in a way that will bring your financial program tumbling down.

When you have learned how to control your income, your expenses, and your debt level . . . you will *automatically* begin to generate surplus funds on a regular basis. You will have extra cash at the end of the month. You will be ready to start investing your capital.

5. YOUR ASSETS (INVESTMENTS, THINGS YOU CAN SELL)

Financial security depends on accumulating things you can sell to other people. You will always want to know the real value of your total assets. This is important because it gives you an idea of where you are right now. The more assets you have to sell, the greater your surplus of resources and the more options you have available to you. Assets are anything you can find a buyer for. Those assets that are immediately salable (cash in the bank, stocks, bonds, etc.) are sometimes called "liquid assets," because they are immediately salable. Assets that may take longer to sell, such as real estate, are called fixed assets.

Your principal objective in managing your assets is to be aware of both the value of your assets and of the reinvestment opportunities that may pay a higher rate of return. Your objective is to balance risk against return to give you the investment program that works best for you.

During the rest of this program we are going to show you techniques you can use to successfully start building your financial estate right now—strategies, skills, planning, and tips you can use to manage the five financial areas we have just covered.

6. YOUR REWARDS

Many people make the mistake of overlooking the daily rewards in life in their haste to reach a long-term goal. Often the constant denial of immediate rewards eventually slows down the momentum and ultimately defeats the long-term project entirely.

It is important for you to continuously monitor the rewards you and the rest of your family are getting on a daily basis. These rewards can range from financial ones (going out to a movie or dinner, vacations, buying luxury items) to psychological and emotional benefits (spending more time together, sharing things together, responding to another's need for affection, warmth, and understanding).

Paying yourself and your family rewards can be an extremely pleasurable experience. By using your imagination to create reward opportunities, you can develop a laundry list of interesting things to do which will add excitement to your daily lives. Often you can replace old habit patterns that cost money (smoking, drinking, gambling) with new patterns that don't (walking, hiking, reading, joining a local theater group, sketching).

Be careful to keep plenty of small rewards coming along regularly so that your life pays off on a daily basis. This gives you a chance to enjoy your life now while still working your way toward long-term goals.

For most of us, earning rewards of one sort or another is the primary motivation for managing our money successfully. Therefore, before you deny yourself something you would enjoy right now, weigh your immediate pleasure against what you will expect to get someday in the future. Usually, you will be able to strike a reasonable balance between short-term and long-term rewards for yourself and your family.

SELECTING YOUR OWN MONEY MANAGEMENT STRATEGY

The key to your long-term success as a money manager will depend on how well you set up systems to measure your progress toward your money management objectives. By now it should be clear that the first step toward becoming a skilled money manager is to create your own set of measuring tools.

Checkbooks and savings accounts measure how much money you have available and how you have spent the money you have. Stock and bond certificates measure how much you have invested in long-term capital investments. Your mortgage balance measures how much you owe on your house.

Managing money is being able to know consistently

where you are at now, where you want to go, and what you have to do to get there.

Some people create elaborate, complicated systems to measure their financial progress. It's up to you how much or how little time you want to spend keeping records. However, there are a few important records we recommend everyone keep. One of these basic records is the Money Management Strategy Chart.

WHAT IS THE MONEY MANAGEMENT STRATEGY CHART?

We have created a form you can use to chart or identify your immediate, five-year, and retirement goals. (See the sample at the end of this chapter.)

The principal objective of this chart is to give you an idea of *where* you want to go. The time you take filling it out is well invested, because it gives you a chance to think about where you are now and where you want to be.

After you have completed your Money Management Strategy Chart, you will have a list of objectives in your hand and an itinerary which highlights the things you want to happen in your life.

HOW TO FILL OUT YOUR MONEY MANAGEMENT STRATEGY CHART

The primary objective of your money management strategy chart is to give you a quick way to list your financial objectives. In the next lesson we will get into the reprogramming process, and you will learn why it is extremely important for you to identify for your internal computer where it is you want to go—in other words, your objectives.

It is important at this time not to worry about *how* you

Money Management Strategy Chart

FINANCIAL OBJECTIVE	IMMEDIATE	FIVE-YEAR	RETIREMENT

will be able to get where it is you would like to go. We will cover that in Lesson 7. Right now, focus your attention on the things you would like to have come into your life right now (immediately), in five years, and when you retire.

As you fill out your strategy chart, don't anguish over it or spend too much time making your decisions. Make it fun. Imagine that you can bring into your life whatever it is you really want. If you *could* do something, what would it be? If you could earn any amount of money, how much would it be?

Filling out your strategy chart is like making a list of countries and cities you want to visit on a trip to Europe. At first, you know there are a few cities you really want to see so you write them down. Then you think of some other places you'd like to go to. Finally, you decide how much time you will have and then you plan your trip accordingly. Usually, you have to eliminate a few of the places you have written down, because there wouldn't be enough time to visit every city in Europe. Financial planning involves the same process. Few of us can do everything we would like to do in a single lifetime, so we focus on one or two things we can get done.

After you have completed your Money Management Strategy Chart, you will have an important document you can use to start controlling the direction of your financial future. But remember, what you have written down can easily be changed. Just because you have set an immediate five-year objective today doesn't mean you can't change it to another one tomorrow.

The sample strategy chart has been filled out to give you an idea of the kind of objectives you may want to aim at in your own life.

Your strategy chart should be looked at frequently to see if you continue to want the objectives you have set for yourself. All of us are constantly changing our attitudes.

What you felt you wanted five years ago may not be important to you anymore. So you will more than likely change your strategy chart from time to time.

The primary objective of your strategy chart is to give you a quick and easy way to check:

1. Where you are now
2. Where you want to be now
3. Where you want to be five years from now
4. Where you want to be when you retire

Once you have taken time to complete your strategy chart, you will begin to find it much easier to manage your money effectively. Planning will also become much easier.

Turn now to Section 5 of your Personality Profile. The objective of this final section of your Personality Profile is to identify the specific financial goals you want to set for yourself. By completing this section, you should come up with the objectives you need to complete your Money Management Strategy Chart. After you have completed your Personality Profile, complete your Money Management Strategy Chart.

The sample on the following page shows you how to do so. Select areas in which you have decided you want to set specific financial goals. (For example, you now live in a $50,000 house and would like to live in a $100,000 house.) Then select the appropriate planning area in which to place that goal (immediate, five-year, retirement).

When you have finished your strategy chart, you will have written down exactly what it is you want to achieve over the coming years. Once you know what it is you want, you can change plans to achieve your objectives. And that's what successful money management is all about.

DO NOT GO ON TO LESSON 6 UNTIL TOMORROW.

SAMPLE

Money Management Strategy Chart

FINANCIAL OBJECTIVE	IMMEDIATE	FIVE-YEAR	RETIREMENT
1. Buy A $100,000 House		X	
2. HAVE $8,000 in Savings Account	X		
3. Buy A Camper	X		
4. Own Income Property			X
5. Annual Income of $25,000/year	X		
6. Monthly Income of $1,500			X
7. 8-week Trip To Europe		X	
8. Develop Executive's Attitude	X		

PERSONALITY PROFILE

SECTION 5
SELECTING YOUR OWN MONEY MANAGEMENT STRATEGY

1. Fill in the blanks to the following questions. Each answer asks for an estimate of a sum of money (for example, the value of your house now and the value of the house you would like to be living in). Don't spend too long thinking about the answers. Try to be realistic, but don't feel you have to be precisely accurate. These projections are designed to give you an idea of where you are now and how far away you are from where you want to be.
2. Estimate the value of the following assets. In the second column put down the value of assets you would like to have right now. Be realistic. Select a figure you are willing to work to achieve.

ASSETS	NOW	WOULD LIKE NOW
1. Annual Salary (If two people work, combine the salary figure.)	______________	______________

ASSETS	NOW	WOULD LIKE NOW
2. Savings	____	____
3. Investments		
a. stocks	____	____
b. bonds	____	____
c. real estate other than your house	____	____
d. other	____	____
4. Insurance		
a. life	____	____
b. disability	____	____
c. health	____	____
5. Household		
a. rent	____	____
b. value, if owned	____	____
6. Other assets		
a. automobile	____	____
b. pension funds	____	____
c. collections, antiques paintings, etc.	____	____
d. other	____	____

3. Estimate your monthly expenses. In the second column put down the amount of money you would like to be able to spend in these areas if you had the money.

MONTHLY EXPENSES	NOW	WOULD LIKE NOW
1. Investments		
a. savings	________	________
b. stocks	________	________
c. bonds	________	________
d. real estate	________	________
e. other	________	________
2. Real Estate		
a. rent/mortgage payment	________	________
b. utilities	________	________
c. household operations	________	________
d. home improvement loans	________	________
e. taxes	________	________
3. Insurance		
a. life	________	________
b. health	________	________
c. disability	________	________
d. liability, theft, homeowner's, etc.	________	________
e. auto	________	________
4. Transportation		

MONTHLY EXPENSES	NOW	WOULD LIKE NOW
a. auto loans	______	______
b. gas/oil	______	______
c. repairs	______	______
5. Food	______	______
6. Clothing	______	______
7. Medical		
a. doctor	______	______
b. dentist	______	______
c. pharmacy	______	______
8. Taxes		
a. with-holding	______	______
b. social security	______	______
9. Telephone	______	______
10. Recreation		
a. vacations	______	______
b. travel	______	______
c. enter-taining	______	______
d. hobbies/sports	______	______
e. other	______	______
11. Special Projects		
a. trip to Europe, new camera, etc.	______	______

MONTHLY EXPENSES	NOW	WOULD LIKE NOW
12. Emergencies	______	______
13. Other Expenses	______	______
14. Cash Left Over	______	______
TOTAL MONTHLY EXPENSES	______	______
TOTAL MONTHLY INCOME	______	______
DIFFERENCE (+ or −)	______	______

HOW TO EVALUATE YOUR PERSONALITY PROFILE

Depending on how experienced you already are with money, this section may be more or less difficult for you to use successfully.

What you are filling out here is essentially a balance sheet—the financial form corporations use to determine their net worth—and a profit and loss statement—the financial form corporations use to track their cash flow.

Be careful not to get too involved with the questions asked here. If you can't come up with immediate answers to one or more of these questions, don't worry about it.

What you are doing here is starting your financial planning on a sound basis. Keep your eye on the money goals you are aiming for rather than the bookkeeping you are using right now to track your progress.

You may discover that this kind of activity interests you and you may want to take a night course in bookkeeping or financial management. You may want to employ an accountant to set up your record-keeping program and assist you with your tax preparation. Or you may simply wish to keep the whole process informal, taking care to use your own judgment to improve your cash flow and capital position.

Whatever plan you select, the important things are to be aware of the process of managing your money successfully and to realize that your understanding of this money process can go a long way toward eliminating many of the money problems that continue to plague more and more families as inflation and increased energy costs combine to reduce the value you are able to get out of the money you have.

LESSON 6

REPROGRAMMING YOUR ATTITUDE TOWARD MONEY

When all else is lost, the future still remains.
—Bovee

You are now about to cover the most important material in this program—reprogramming.

Up to this point, we have been covering the mechanical process of organizing and managing money. From time to time, when we went beyond the mechanics into the psychology of money, we said that the psychological changes you may need to make will be discussed in the reprogramming section of this program.

Reprogramming is the behavior modification process we have developed to give you a chance to change your thinking and behavior patterns. Please take time to study this 7-step reprogramming technique. It is the technique you can use to reprogram your ideas and habits as you grow older so that you are not continually stuck in the habits and thinking you developed earlier in your life. Reprogramming can be your ticket to personal freedom. Once you are free of the restrictive patterns that your old, automatic programs impose on you, you can open up enormous options in your life and a chance for continued personal growth.

After you have mastered the reprogramming process, you can use it in every area of your life. You can use it to reprogram habits you no longer want, to change your attitudes about yourself, your environment, your goals, your agreements—everything that influences the way you live. Reprogramming is an extremely valuable asset for you to have and one that you will find yourself using over and over again after you have mastered it.

WHY?

It is one thing to know where you want to go, it is another thing to get there—especially if it requires a major change in your thinking and behavior patterns.

There is a story about a golfer who had the best strokes of anyone on the professional tour. Everything worked, his woods, his irons, his putting. He knew everything about the game and his practice rounds were generally lower than any of the other golfers. But when he got into competition it was a different story. Things went wrong. Errors occurred. He never won a major tournament during his career. When asked why this happened he answered, "I know how to play the best game of golf on the tour. I just can't seem to be able to *do* it."

Knowing is one thing, doing is something else. You can read every book in the world about tennis. You can watch all the important players play tennis. You can become the world's greatest expert on tennis. But you can't *play* tennis until you decide to pick up a raquet and get out on a court and start hitting a tennis ball. Unfortunately, this is the point at which many of us turn down opportunities to do new things. We may do all our homework, but we are reluctant to take the risk of jumping into a new game. There are many reasons why we do this. Sometimes we are afraid we will look foolish. Sometimes we have developed an *image* of ourselves which doesn't allow us to try different, out-of-character roles. In a lot of cases, we have *programmed* ourselves to act in a certain way and find it extremely difficult to do something that doesn't fit this program.

Perhaps the hardest skill to learn is how to bring about a significant change in our thinking and behavior patterns. And yet, without this skill we will be stuck in the programs that have already taken over our lives, many of which were programmed into us during our childhood. It is this frustrating state of being stuck in a program we don't like—excessive drinking, smoking, shyness, overreacting, poor money management habits—that causes many of us to give up trying anything new or different.

But there are ways we can change ourselves. People do stop smoking. People do lose weight. People do become successful money managers. Usually, it is not easy to reprogram yourself, especially the first time you try to do so. Some people require the help of a psychotherapist to bring about changes in their lives, and that's OK. But in almost all cases, people who learn how to change their thinking and behavior patterns do so by learning and carrying out a strategy that works for them.

REPROGRAMMING, A STRATEGY FOR CHANGE

After you have evaluated your present financial situation, you will be able to see how far you are from where you want to be. You may discover that you are already there. Fine! Keep it up!

However, you may discover that where you want to be is impossible or requires too much effort (you are forty-five years old and want to play starting quarterback for the Los Angeles Rams). Accept this interest as a daydream or fantasy; enjoy it, but look around for a realistic goal you *can* achieve—such as being a coach for a Pop Warner football team.

In many cases, you will discover that you have not yet reached your objectives. In order to do so, you will have to bring about some important changes in your thinking and behavior patterns.

This can be a very difficult thing to do because it means you have to break habits that have become imprinted onto your internal computer. And these habits get more firmly entrenched as you get older. You can become aware of the habits you want to change, but you don't seem to be able to make these changes. (You *want* to stop smoking but you can't do it—the habit is firmly fixed into your patterns.) That's why most "self-help" programs fail.

In order to help you break these patterns, we have developed a 7-step process we call reprogramming. Our brain is very much like the computers we are using today to manage many of the things going on in our world. Just as we can change the activities of the computers, we can change our own activities by reprogramming our own computer. We can substitute a "non-smoking" program for our old "smoking" program. We can change or modify those programs that are getting in our way with new ones that will help us get where we want to go.

OUR INTERNAL COMPUTER

Our brain is like an analog computer. The main characteristic of an analog computer is that it is self-correcting. It can learn to make adjustments in small increments and correct itself so that the next pattern reflects the modified program. This is how we learn to ride a bicycle. If you lean too far to one side, you compensate by leaning to the other side. When you are just beginning to learn a new skill, you often "overcorrect" and fall down.

As you practice a new skill, you begin to get better at it, and you fall down less frequently. We call this process "failing successfully." Eventually, with enough practice you will reach your level of potential in that skill area. All along the way your internal computer will be adjusting itself to master the new skill. Finally, after you have practiced long enough, the "automatic" mode of your internal computer will take over. You will have programmed a set of thinking and behavior patterns into your computer that now becomes essentially automatic. You find that you can be thinking of other things while you are doing this activity. (How many times, for example, have you been driving your car and thinking about something else almost as if you were asleep? Suddenly you find yourself at your destination almost without realizing it.) At this point, your program has become a *habit.*

These automatic habits or programs are vital to our survival. If we were not able to store these programs in our internal computer, we would have to relearn every skill each time we wanted to use it. So when you find yourself following an automatic pattern—such as smoking or drinking—don't think of it as a sign of weakness, because it isn't; it is a sign of strength, a kind of internal conscience. Your automatic programs are working well. When you run up against an old automatic program that you don't want

THE REPROGRAMMING PROCESS

Identify the old program you want to change.

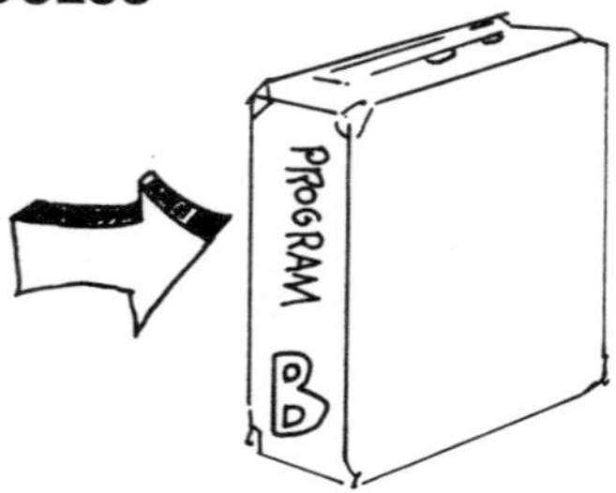

Write down the new program you want to follow.

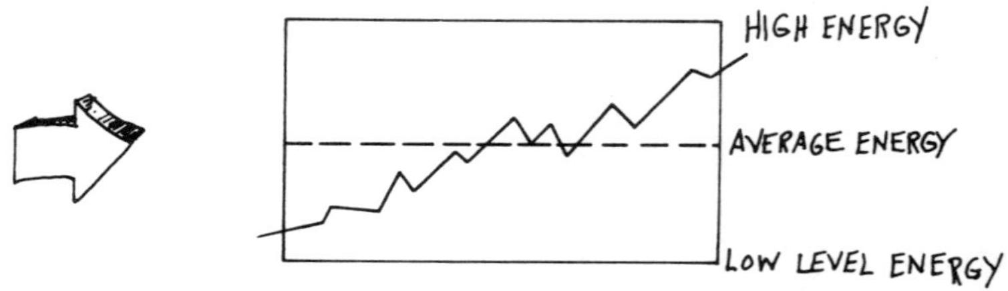

Bring your energy level up to its maximum potential.

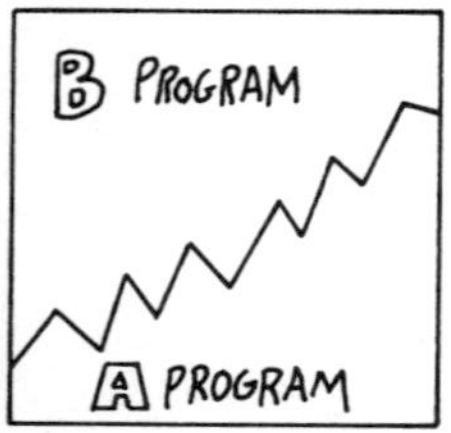

Practice your new B-Program.

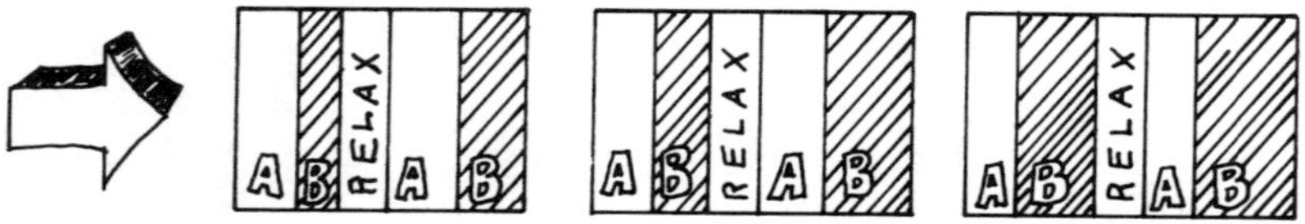

FAIL SUCCESSFULLY. Accept the conflict going on between your old A-Program and your new B-Program. Back off when you feel anxious or uncomfortable. Be patient. Don't force change.

Enjoy experiencing your new B-Program.

Use REPROGRAMMING to modify your thinking and behavior patterns so

anymore, what you have to do is reprogram it into a program that will get you the behavior pattern you do want.

THE REPROGRAMMING PROCESS

Study the illustration on the preceding page to get a general idea how the reprogramming process works. Then take as much time as you need to thoroughly understand this process. Be sure to keep relaxed as you start practicing reprogramming. Make a game out of it. Reward yourself often. Take plenty of time to master reprogramming. It is a good idea to start out by reprogramming a small, relatively unimportant program you would like to change, rather than tackling one of your major problem areas. For example, you could start reprogramming yourself to wake up on time every morning rather than starting out by trying to reprogram your smoking habit.

STEP 1: BECOME AWARE OF YOUR OLD BEHAVIOR PATTERNS

The first step in the reprogramming process is to become aware of the old behavior patterns you wish to change. As we have said, you can use reprogramming to make significant changes in any part of your life. In terms of managing your money, there are many ways you might wish to use reprogramming. You could . . .

- change your attitude toward money to the millionaire's attitude.
- overcome your fear of large amounts of money.
- change a habit (smoking, drinking, overeating) which is draining money out of your income.

To make it easier for you to follow the 7-step process, we have selected a single example to use as we describe the reprogramming process. Let's imagine you are a person who finds it impossible not to tip waiters or waitresses in a restaurant no matter how bad the food or service may be. You find that no matter how much you don't want to tip a waiter or a waitress, you feel compelled to tip 15%; that is your existing behavior pattern.

You uncover a behavior pattern and you become aware of it by observing what the pattern is. In this case you observe that you always tip 15% of any bill that you pay in any restaurant, coffee shop, or anyplace you go out of your house to order food.

This isn't a major problem in your life, but it is a behavior pattern you would like to change. The first step is becoming aware of this behavior pattern. For the purposes of this reprogramming process, let's define your behavior patterns as those things that you can see yourself doing. Think of a behavior pattern as something you could take a motion picture of or make a television tape of. It must be a behavior pattern you can see yourself doing. We want to separate the thinking patterns from the behavior patterns so that you can more easily master this reprogramming process.

To sum up, you have determined that every time you dine out, no matter what the quality of the service, you always tip 15%. This is the first step of the reprogramming process. You have now become aware of a behavior pattern, and you have identified it. You should now write down on a piece of paper what that behavior pattern is.

When you have completed step 1, you will have written, "The behavior pattern I wish to change is the fact that I always tip 15% whenever I dine out."

STEP 2: BECOME AWARE OF YOUR OLD THINKING PATTERNS

Observe yourself as you implement or carry out these behavior patterns. When you go out to a restaurant or a coffee shop, detach yourself from what you're doing, take yourself off "automatic," and think about the emotional reasons why you are doing this particular thing. For example, try to analyze why it is you tip 15%. Is it because you're embarrassed not to tip? Is it because you're afraid that the waiter or the waitress will react negatively if you don't tip? Can you remember an experience in your past in which someone embarrassed you because you did not tip 15%? Do you recall that your father or mother always tipped 15% and told you to follow the same principles?

During this step your objective is to determine what influences you as you carry out this behavior pattern. You will try to discover the emotional or personal reasons you are doing this and the emotional attitudes or feelings you have toward tipping 15%. Why do you do it? What rewards do you think you are getting from this particular set of behavior patterns? What might happen if you didn't carry out this behavior pattern?

Take a separate piece of paper and write down all the reasons why you think you are carrying out this behavior pattern, and you will now be more aware of some of the reasons why you adopted this pattern. We call these sets of behavior and thinking patterns your "A-Program."

Your A-Program is the existing program you desire to replace on your internal computer. The first two steps of the reprogramming process enable you to identify this specific A-Program, isolate it from the other programs on your internal computer, and determine what it is you want to change and what elements make it up.

STEP 3: CREATE YOUR NEW B-PROGRAM

You are now ready to select the new program you want to substitute for the old program you are now following.

In the example we are using, you have now decided you no longer want to automatically tip 15% of every bill that you receive when you dine out. This is your A-Program, and now it is necessary to create a new program to replace it.

We call this new program your "B-Program." Your B-Program is the new set of thinking and behavior patterns you have decided you want to use from this point forward. It is important in setting up your new B-Program that you do not set up a negative program.

You should not write up a new program that says, "I will not tip 15% anymore in restaurants." (And you should not replace an old smoking program with a new program that says, "I won't smoke anymore.")

Develop a positive, constructive program to aim at and not a negative program, which is something you are attempting to stop yourself from doing. In this example, let's assume you write down on a third sheet of paper the following B-Program:

B-PROGRAM FOR TIPPING:

I desire to have control over my emotions and behavior patterns when I dine out. Because I believe that the quality of service around the country is generally deteriorating because everybody automatically tips 15% on their bills, and because I want to reward those waiters and waitresses who give me better service, I will tip what I want to and where I want to. I will be able to save money on those bills that reflect poor service or poor food. Sometimes I will tip more than

> 15% to those waiters or waitresses who give me superior service. This frees me from an automatic habit pattern, makes my life more enjoyable, and gives me more control over my money. I am making choices for my behavior.

This new program is your B-Program. It is with this set of attitudes and behaviors that you will be working to replace your old program.

You have now completed the third reprogramming step. You now have in writing two separate programs. One is the old program you no longer want to use, and the other is the new program you do want to use and develop. Now it is necessary to actually go through the physical process of reprogramming your internal computer so you can change your thinking and behavior from the old pattern into the new one.

STEP 4: BECOME AWARE OF THE STATE OF YOUR PHYSICAL HEALTH

This is a step many behavior modification programs overlook, yet this step is absolutely vital to your success. In order for you to be able to successfully practice the technique of reprogramming, you must be certain that you are in good physical and mental/emotional condition. If you are not in good condition, your body will not possess the energy you need to achieve your objectives.

If your physical condition is run down, this is a situation you should change in order to be able to count on sufficient energy to achieve your reprogramming objectives. Each of us is an energy producing machine. We all possess a certain degree of physical and mental resources, which we use to survive. Many of the situations we perceive as problems in our lives come from the fact that we are out of condition

—mentally and/or physically run down. We aren't able to sustain our concentration, enthusiasm, or motivation to work on changes.

We will not suggest a specific program to bring your energy level, or general level of health, up to its maximum potential, but we do suggest that if you feel you are not in good physical and mental shape, you check with your physician and design a physical exercise program, a diet program, and a nutritional program to improve your physical condition. If you are seriously out of shape either physically or emotionally, it may be better for you to postpone your specific reprogramming goal until you have raised your energy level to a state that is sufficient to provide you with the resources you need.

You must also learn some simple relaxation techniques to help you calm down if you feel anxious or tense. Relaxation is a part of being in good enough shape to make changes in your thinking and behavior patterns.

STEP 5: PRACTICING YOUR NEW B-PROGRAM

In the beginning, as you practice your new reprogramming process, you may find it difficult to keep yourself from automatically reverting to your old A-Program. This happens frequently.

Without consciously thinking about what you're doing, you may find yourself automatically reverting to your old A-Program every time you're in a situation that triggers this old program. In other words, if you are not aware of what you're doing, you may find that you walk into a restaurant and automatically tip 15% and leave the restaurant without ever thinking about it.

It is necessary for you to practice your new B-Program, and this will take conscious awareness on your part. Every time you go into a restaurant from now on, you are going to have to remind yourself what your new B-Program is. Take yourself off automatic, and be sure that you are practicing your new program and not your old one. You may have to take time to *stop, look,* and *listen* to your behavior.

You may also find it difficult to do the new program. You may find that the same thinking pattern which caused you "automatically" to tip 15% may cause you some anxiety—anxiety which can result in a reversion to the A-Program. For example, you may walk into a restaurant and get poor service yet still find yourself tipping 15% because you are afraid of what the waiter or the waitress might say if you don't.

This is why you are practicing your new technique. Your objective is to continually practice your new program, relaxing when you feel tense until you find that *not* tipping creates no more appreciable anxiety and you are able to carry out your new program without finding it too difficult or too uncomfortable to do so.

It is important to continue to practice your new B-Program, even though you may find yourself failing to complete it. This leads us to step 6 in the reprogramming process.

STEP 6: FAIL SUCCESSFULLY

You will find that as you practice your new B-Program, you will fail from time to time. For example, you will walk into a restaurant, you will get bad service, and you will say to yourself, "I am not going to tip anything this time." But then, when the bill comes and the waiter or waitress is staring you in the eye, you find that you go ahead and tip the usual 15% anyway.

You are now *failing successfully.* The difference between failing and failing successfully is the fact that you now have an objective toward which you are heading. Your new B-Program is written out and you understand what it is. You are working at it. Therefore, when you fail to completely carry out your new program and revert to your old program you are not really failing—you are working on making the changes. It's part of the plan—working toward the new program.

This is true because every time you break the automatic part of the pattern that has been driving you in the past, even though you are not actually physically able to complete the new program, you are removing a little bit of the power the old program has over you. (Your analog computer is slowly self-correcting itself to your new program.) And you are desensitizing yourself to the potential tension and discomfort that can be there when you don't do your old A-Program as it has been scheduled. You are telling your internal computer you no longer want to carry out the old program. You are slowly reprogramming your old A-Program. So don't get discouraged when you fail in your efforts to carry out your new program. Try to relax, reduce the tension, and re-enter the arena to try again . . . and again. Slowly and step by step.

HANDLING STRESS AND ANXIETY

As you begin to practice your new B-Program, especially if it involves a major shift in your thinking and behavior patterns, the chances are that you are going to experience moments of anxiety, nervousness, stress, and panic. This is natural and reasonable and part of the process of change. This happens to almost all of us when we are stepping out into the unknown, into a new area with which we are unfamiliar.

It is important for you to be aware that you may be feeling these tensions and that it is natural to do so. It is also helpful to have a strategy you can use to deal with this stress.

We recommend that you visualize a scale of discomfort or tension that goes from 0 (zero) to 5 (five), with 5 being a state of very high anxiety and discomfort. When you start to practice your new B-Program, monitor the degree of discomfort, stress, or anxiety you are experiencing. When you start to reach midpoint on the scale (around 2 or 3) back off, take a moment out, and relax. Take two steps backward and let that opportunity to practice your new B-Program go by.

Take a moment off from your learning process. Do it deliberately and intentionally. It's a small failure because at that moment you have reached your limit in practicing that part of your learning process. And that's OK, because you are *stretching* your new skills slowly on a step by step basis.

After you have relaxed, move back into the situation again and practice your new B-Program again up to the point where it looks like it is getting away from you. Go in and out until you maintain a satisfactory 1–2 level all the way through the practice.

HOW TO KNOW WHEN YOU ARE REACHING YOUR OWN STRESS LIMIT

There are some pretty standard things that will begin to happen when you are pushing yourself into the high-stress limits. You may begin to notice your pulse rate increasing significantly, and you may begin to feel the physical symptoms of anxiety, tension, and stress. These symptoms may include a flushed face, a rapid heartbeat, a tightness in your body, a dryness in your mouth, or a little lightheadedness. It is possible you may feel not really grounded at that moment; things might start to move too quickly for you. You don't feel relaxed, pleasant, comfortable, or in control of things. You may find that you lose sight of your objective for the moment. You may begin to think, "Why did I get myself into this in the first place. Where is my old familiar A-Program?"

Your desire to return to your old patterns may become so overpowering and compelling that you find yourself actually turning back to your old A-Program. (You start stuffing yourself in front of the refrigerator, smoking twice as much as normal, or drinking far more than usual.)

Try to back off before you reach that point and allow yourself to revert to the old A-Program if that's what comes up. Tell yourself, "OK, I've reached my stress limit this time and so I'm going to let myself do the old A-program." Or just stop and don't do anything.

At first, you may find yourself going too far, beyond the point where you can resist the old A-Program. You may have waited too long and gotten into the 4 or 5 range of your stress level . . . and then automatically into the A-Program. That's a sign you've waited too long to step back. But that's also a sign you are failing successfully, because now you are aware of what is happening to you. Make a note of how far you went, and the next time practice backing off before you reach that stress level.

By practicing your new B-Program this way, you will be handling your stress effectively while at the same time practicing your new program. So you are slowly clearing away the unknown and getting closer to experiencing your new program. By taking your time, rewarding yourself, and pulling back before your stress level gets too high, you will be mastering the process of changing without exceeding the level of risk you are comfortable in taking.

Be inventive and creative in practicing this process. For example, you may not want to practice your new tipping program at a business lunch with important clients in your favorite restaurant. Instead, practice it when you are out of town on a business trip and eating alone. You may want to take some time at first and practice seeing through an imaginary scene or two—at your convenience.

Once you have mastered this process, you may want to try "jumping in" to a new B-Program just to see what stress level may occur. This is called implosive learning. For example, a person wants to swim so he or she jumps into the deep end of the pool and sees what happens. Sometimes it works, but more often than not he or she sinks to the bottom of the pool or gets panicky. So don't be surprised to find that you really do need to take your new learning in a step-by-step fashion, gradually taking time to make your new behavior patterns work for you.

It is really a testing process just like learning to drive a car. You are developing a new skill (i.e., driving) and you are making sure that you learn the skill slowly and with minimum risk. (For example, you practice driving on a country road and not Los Angeles Freeway.)

STEP 7: EXPERIENCE YOUR NEW B-PROGRAM AT WORK

One day you will be able to walk into a restaurant, get poor service, and without a second thought simply refuse to leave a tip. If the waiter or waitress makes any comment, you will simply remark that the service and/or the food was below the standard you have set for yourself, and unless it's improved you will not tip. When your B-Program is worked into your internal computer, you will be able to do this easily, without much anxiety if any. It will be the program *you* have selected as your choice, and you will have learned how to integrate this program into your system. If you persist in your reprogramming process, eventually your new B-Program will take over on "automatic."

You will find that you're rarely failing successfully anymore. In fact, you may have stopped your old A-Program altogether; no longer will you tip 15% automatically, everywhere you go. Your new behavior patterns will reflect precisely those patterns you have programmed into your computer.

SUMMARY

You have the option of programming yourself as you want. You have the potential to restructure your behavior and thinking patterns so that they work for you, not against you. No matter how tough your life may have become, this can be true for you. No matter how many bad breaks or disappointments you may have had, no matter how low you may have sunk financially, physically, mentally, or emotionally—you can use this reprogramming process to begin to build a better life for yourself over the coming months and years. You have taken over an active part in choosing what you want to happen in your life, and you now have a process that can significantly assist you in implementing your choices. Practice it!

A RELAXATION TECHNIQUE PROCESS

During your reprogramming, you are going to want to master the technique of relaxation. The following is a process you can use to learn to relax. Practice it until you have mastered it and you will receive continued personal benefits.

Take a fifteen-minute period of time when you can lie down or sit comfortably and quietly in a chair where you won't be disturbed by the telephone or other people. Take a minute to feel what it is like to just sit there and not have to do anything. Be aware of the feelings and sensations in your body. Be aware of any tightness or tension in your muscles. If you notice any sounds or thoughts that tend to distract you, put them aside for the moment. Don't focus on them. They are there . . . it's just that you aren't going to pay attention to them at this point in time.

NOW . . . breathe in very deeply . . . hold your breath for five seconds . . . then *slowly* exhale and be aware of the tension gradually releasing as you exhale. Wait ten seconds; enjoy the rest. Now once again inhale very deeply . . . hold it . . . then breathe out again and notice the increase in relaxation and the release in tension. DO THIS 3–5 TIMES. Be aware of the release of tightness and tension as you exhale. Take the moment right after exhaling to enjoy and appreciate the release of tension all through your body.

Think about any tension or tightness in the different parts of your body—arms, legs, neck, back, shoulders, facial muscles, etc. Practice focusing your attention on a particular part of your body and then breathe and relax that part. Do this thoroughly. While you are following this procedure, think to yourself, "I am relaxing . . . I feel relaxed in my arms, legs, stomach . . ."

Your mind will come to associate the idea of relaxation and the reduction of tension in your body. Thinking and feeling are closely related. As you think about relaxing, you will gradually learn to relax more and more. Soon just thinking about relaxing will be coupled with the feeling of relaxation. You will develop more of an automatic response. But you need to practice.

Practice this procedure regularly. The first week do the exercises daily. It is important to practice for a week or so before trying to apply this in your reprogramming sessions. After the initial learning of the relaxation technique, continue to practice the exercises two to three times a week for ten minutes each session. During times of stress and crisis you will want to practice these procedures even more frequently in order to keep up your ability to relax when you want to.

A good way to relax your entire system is to take a couple of minutes when you are sitting quietly and picture in your imagination some place that is especially refreshing and pleasant for you, a setting that really contributes to your feeling of well-being. Try to picture as many details of this place as you can. What is it like to be there? What are the sights, sounds, smells? Really try to create the sensation of being there for a few minutes. Take it all in. Add it to your state of physical relaxation at the time. Tell yourself: "I feel relaxed to be here."

Together, the mental and physical states can add up to a great degree of total tension reduction. Think of this process as RELAXATION. Have that word as your cue for the feeling of being at ease and for the reduction of apprehension and tension.

So when you say to yourself, "relax," you can recapture the state of tension reduction by breathing slowly and deeply, allowing a quick flash of your imaginary relaxation scene to come through. Then appreciate the easing of the tightness and apprehension that has been present.

DO NOT GO ON TO LESSON 7 UNTIL TOMORROW.

LESSON 7

CREATING YOUR OWN MONEY PLAN

Bait your hook an' keep on tryin'.
Keep a-goin'.
—Frank L. Stanton

Action is the key difference between success and failure in whatever you do. A lot of people dream about making changes, but get all hung up in the "dreaming." A lot of people wish for change in their lives and stop there. If you seriously want to make some changes in your life, you've got to take that first *action step.*

If you don't take it, nobody else is really going to take it for you. You can fool yourself all your life by laying what is happening to you off on other people—your parents, your children, your wife or husband, your employer, your country, your world—but the only person being fooled is yourself.

It is sometimes frightening to take these action steps, especially if you are insecure or afraid of what might happen. You can overcome this inaction and fear by developing your own action plan, which anticipates what you are going to do and what will happen after you do it. This transforms the "unknown" in your life to the "known" and gives you a method you can use to measure your progress.

Planning is an important skill that most people misunderstand, because they have zeroed in on the "paper work" of planning while forgetting what the real objective of planning is. You are already a natural planner. Every day in your life you do hundreds of things that work out exactly the way you expect them to. Many of these things you do without even thinking about them. By taking this skill you already have and applying it to money, you can experience dramatic results.

Your new plan will become your means to change your life into what you want it to be. As you practice this planning process and become more proficient at it, you will become more confident. After a while you won't be wondering what it is you can do to make your life more rewarding and exciting, but rather which of several opportunities you want to select.

Your planning will keep you headed in the right direction —on course—so that you can make progress toward achieving realistic goals while avoiding the traps that often keep others from succeeding.

A REVIEW

Before you get into creating your own money management plan, let's review what we have covered so far.

Successful money managing is a process. In order to manage your money successfully, you continually monitor the things that are going on—internally and externally. Managing money isn't just dealing with the dollars that come through your checking account but a process which enables you to discover and attain your specific financial objectives in life.

Therefore, the most important thing you must do is understand yourself. This means you must understand what your attitudes toward money are now, and you must be able to learn how to change attitudes that are standing in your way.

In this lesson we are going to suggest a planning process you can use to accomplish your financial objectives.

PLANNING YOUR WAY TO INDEPENDENCE

The principal benefit of planning is to give yourself a written objective and a series of proposed action steps designed to achieve that objective. A good plan is like a road map: It shows the final destination and usually marks the best way to get there, depending on what it is you want to do.

It's not only important to know where you want to go but how you want to get there. For example, two different people may want to drive from San Francisco to Los Angeles. One of them might be going to Los Angeles to apply for a job. The objective is to get there immediately, as soon as possible, to land that job. So he or she will select the quickest way to get to Los Angeles by car.

The other person might be on a three-week vacation. This person wants to drive to Los Angeles slowly on the most beautiful roads, stopping often to see the interesting sights, spending several nights in quaint inns along the way, and touring the area between the two cities.

Both people have the same destination but for different reasons. It is important to keep this in mind, because there isn't really any single way to get from one place to another.

Each person has different objectives, desires, strengths, and weaknesses. That's why general systems for managing money or playing tennis or cooking often fail to work as well as you might hope they would. In the end, we all have to take the time and energy to develop our own personal "road map" through life.

Many people misunderstand the purpose of planning. We think a plan gives you a way to measure your progress toward or away from a stated goal. For example, if you haven't recorded how much money you have already saved and how much more you want to save, how can you determine if you are achieving your savings goal?

Many people set an objective and then live their whole lives in terms of the plan they have selected—whether it works or not! In other words, they let their plans rule their lives. We believe it should be the other way around. Plans should support your life-style. Plans must be flexible. If things aren't working, you have every right to change your plans. Just because you started out for Hawaii on your vacation doesn't mean you can't change your plans and spend it in San Francisco.

This doesn't mean you should change your plans without giving thought to what you are doing. What it does mean is that whatever direction in life you select for yourself, you will probably have a better chance of getting there if you have written down a plan against which you can measure your progress.

So a plan is a road map you follow to get somewhere. If you decide not to go there, you write up a new plan with a new destination, and start out on a different adventure.

THE 6-PART MONEY PLANNING PROCESS

The following money planning process can be used by you to organize your thinking and activities to achieve your money objectives. It is *not* a plan you can follow automatically. In fact, it is not a plan at all! There is absolutely no way we can write your plan for you. Only you can write that plan. This 6-part process shows you how you can write up your plan.

It is important to understand why we just don't give you a prepackaged money management plan. Many books and programs sell this kind of information. You get a 14-step real-estate plan guaranteed to make you a millionaire in three years.

It is true that the person who wrote that "plan" may have used it to make a million in three years, but that's no guarantee that any other person in the world will be able to follow it successfully. The most important part of any plan is the capability, interests, character, skills, talents, judgment, and motivation of the person who is going to have to implement the plan. That's why somebody else's plan almost never works out quite as well when you try to use it for your own.

You can certainly benefit from someone else's experience and avoid the traps that await the amateur in a new venture by becoming informed about what it is you are doing, but in the end you are going to have to walk across the bridge yourself. You are going to have to "go it alone."

PLANNING IS A PROCESS

For this reason, we have given you a process you can use to create your own plan. The plan you create will depend upon who you are and where you want to be and what you are interested in and a lot of other things that only you can know and decide on.

What we have done is to identify the six key areas you are going to have to monitor in order to develop your successful money management plan. By being aware of these areas, you can move forward with confidence and with the knowledge that you are covering the important bases in managing your money. There is no guarantee that even by following this strategy you will succeed in achieving your objectives, but at least you will be aware of the kinds of thinking and activities you should be doing to have a chance for success.

As you begin to develop your own plan, continue to explore each of these six areas until you have defined precisely what it is you want to achieve in each area. As you practice your new skills and as you become more aware of the money management process, you will find it all coming together. The more you study the money process, the better you will understand it and the greater will be your odds for success.

HOW TO COMPLETE YOUR MONEY PLANS

When you filled in your Money Management Strategy Chart, you identified *where* you want to go, or your financial objectives. It is now necessary to determine *how* you are going to get there. Your plans will identify the action steps you should take right now to start you on your way toward achieving the financial objectives you have set. In each of the six money management areas, you have written down one or more specific objectives you want to reach immediately, in five years, or when you retire. You are now ready to work up:

1. Your money attitude plans
2. Your money income plans
3. Your money expense plans
4. Your money debt plans
5. Your money investment plans
6. Your money reward plans

As we have said, planning is a process you use to move from one place to another. The first step to effective planning is to identify precisely where you are right now. Once you know your starting place, you can then identify where it is you want to be. When you know where you want to be, you can then estimate the time, energy, and money it will take you to get there.

Start out by choosing one of the objectives you have written down on your Money Management Strategy Chart. Using a Financial Planning Form (see sample that follows), work up your plans. Look at the sample plans we have completed to get an idea of how you can work up your own.

In each area where you have written down a financial objective, go through the following 4-step process to complete your money plan:

1. Write down your financial objective (where you want to be).
2. Identify where you are now.
3. Ask yourself the following seven questions to determine how you are going to reach your objective:
    a. Do I really want to reach this objective?
    b. Is it a realistic objective for me?
    c. How much time, energy, and money will it take me to get there?
    d. Why do I want to reach this objective?
    e. Will my family and friends support me in working to reach this objective?

f. What will I have to give up to reach this objective?
g. What action steps should I take right now to start heading toward this objective?

4. Immediately begin to take action steps to reach your objective.

Let's use two of the sample objectives we included on the Money Management Strategy Chart in Lesson 5 to demonstrate how to develop a money management plan. The first sample objective will be to develop an executive's attitude toward money.

You would begin by filling out the Financial Planning Form. Take a look at the following sample form.

You should complete a financial plan for each financial objective you want to start working toward now.

The more ambitious your objectives, the more difficult it may be and the longer it may take for you to reach them. That's fine. In some cases, you may not *know* how to reach an objective. For example, you may decide you want to have investments in the amount of $400,000 by the time you retire. At this point you may have no idea how you can achieve this objective. Don't worry about it. If you don't know precisely how to reach one of your objectives, write the following statement (or one of your own) in the section of your plan which outlines your immediate action steps:

> 7. What action steps should I take right now to start heading toward this objective?
>
>   I will continue to explore ways to reach this objective until my internal computer begins to give me ideas as to how I can start achieving this objective.

Don't try to force yourself to come up with an immediate

SAMPLE

Financial Planning Form

Where I Want To Be	Where I Am Now
I want to develop an executive's attitude toward money.	I have a middle-income attitude toward money.

1. DO I REALLY WANT TO REACH THIS OBJECTIVE?
   Yes.
2. IS IT A REALISTIC OBJECTIVE FOR ME?
   Yes.
3. HOW MUCH TIME, ENERGY, AND MONEY WILL IT TAKE ME TO GET THERE?
   I can use reprogramming to develop this new money attitude. It shouldn't take more than a month or so and will cost no money.
4. WHY DO I WANT TO REACH THIS OBJECTIVE?
   It will give me an opportunity to earn more money in the future and it is the attitude I want to have toward money.
5. WILL MY FAMILY AND FRIENDS SUPPORT ME IN REACHING THIS GOAL?
   Yes. However, by keeping my objective to myself I will have a better chance of achieving it in this case.
6. WHAT WILL I HAVE TO GIVE UP TO REACH THIS OBJECTIVE?
   I will have to give up my middle-income attitude.
7. WHAT ACTION STEPS SHOULD I TAKE RIGHT NOW?
   a. I will begin to reprogram my attitude toward money today.
   b. I will begin to explore how executives perceive money: I will subscribe to one or two business magazines (*Fortune, Business Week,* etc.) and I will read books by executives. I will also attend lectures, seminars, and night courses to gain additional insights into how executives perceive money.
   c. If I have trouble changing my attitude, I will ask myself questions like: If I were an executive, what would I think about this? If a successful executive had this problem, how would he or she solve it?
   d. Whenever possible, I will seek the company of successful executives. I will be aware of how they think, talk, dress, act, etc.

answer to a problem you may not be ready to solve. Be patient. Keep your final objective in mind and you will find that sooner or later your internal computer will begin to feed you the information you need.

Let's look at another example from the sample Money Management Strategy Chart and develop a financial plan for it. This time, the objective will be to acquire $8,000 in savings within three years. As you follow this guideline, remember that it is the *process* of examining your objective and developing action steps that is important.

You should review each of your six financial planning areas and select specific objectives you have identified. You should then evaluate where you are right now and estimate the changes you will have to make to get where you want to go.

After you have done this, you will be able to see precisely where you are now. You will be able to see how near or how far away you are from where you want to be.

KEY POINT

> When you have completed one of your financial plans, you may then decide you no longer want to spend the energy, time, money, etc., to get to your original objective. That's OK. Fine! Cross it off your strategy chart and set a new goal for yourself.

GENERAL PLANNING TIPS

The following are general planning tips relating to the process of planning in each of your six financial planning areas. By using some of these tips, you can practice developing your own plans. Remember, you are learning a new skill

SAMPLE

Financial Planning Form

Where I Want To Be	Where I Am Now
I want to have $8,000 in my savings account.	I have $4,500 in my savings account.

1. DO I REALLY WANT TO REACH THIS OBJECTIVE?
   Yes.
2. IS IT A REALISTIC OBJECTIVE FOR ME?
   Yes.
3. HOW MUCH TIME, ENERGY, AND MONEY WILL IT TAKE ME TO GET THERE?
   I need to save an additional $3,500. Right now we are saving about $800 a year. I want to have the $8,000 in three years, so I will have to save $375 more each year. This means I will have to increase my income in some way.
4. WHY DO I WANT TO REACH THIS OBJECTIVE?
   It is the first step toward my overall objective of managing my money so that I can retire comfortably and increase my personal assets and investments. This amount of money will give me a financial cushion should a money crisis come up.
5. WILL MY FAMILY AND FRIENDS SUPPORT ME IN REACHING THIS GOAL?
   Yes, as long as it doesn't take too much time away from being with my wife and children.
6. WHAT WILL I HAVE TO GIVE UP TO REACH THIS OBJECTIVE?
   Perhaps some free time so that I can work part time to increase our income, or some luxury items we might buy.
7. WHAT ACTION STEPS SHOULD I TAKE RIGHT NOW?
   a. I'll review our expenses to see if I can squeeze out an additional $15 a month. This will save $180 a year.
   b. I'll look for a part-time job over Christmas, which should net me the $195 I'll need to reach my goal of $375 for this year. My next raise will cover the difference for the second and third years.

so don't be discouraged if at first it goes slowly and you feel a little lost. Keep practicing. Think of the first few times through as practice runs. If you find yourself getting confused or tense, back off; put your plans away for a while and then come back to them later on.

1. YOUR MONEY ATTITUDE PLANS

Everything begins with your personal, major attitude toward money. As you learned in Section 1 of your Personality Profile, we all have a specific set of programs that have been fed into our internal computer. The result of this is that we end up taking a "position" about money.

By now you will have a good idea of your major attitude toward money. If your attitude is the one you want to continue to have, great! You are already where you want to be.

For example, if you decide you want to follow the middle-income strategy to obtain money and you already have a middle-income attitude toward money, you have no reprogramming to do to change your money attitudes and behavior.

On the other hand, if you decide you want to take the entrepreneur's attitude toward money and right now you have a clerk's attitude, you are going to have to make some changes.

Remember that the millionaire's attitude frees you from money altogether and gives you a money attitude that works for whatever specific financial objectives you decide you want to set for yourself.

When you have completed your money attitude plan you should know where you are, where you want to be, and what changes you will have to make to get there.

2. YOUR MONEY INCOME PLANS

Once you have selected your money attitude, you can determine the income level you want to achieve over the coming years. It's time to decide whether you would prefer to live on a limited income or to take the time and work necessary to become a millionaire.

It is important not to limit your income objective by where you really are right now. You are setting a goal, selecting a destination—the place you want to be. You will see in the next two lessons that each and every one of us can decide we want to become a millionaire if that's what we really want.

But remember that there is a great and important difference between *wanting* to become a millionaire and *wishing* you were a millionaire.

When you want to become a millionaire, you work up a strategy to give you the opportunity to reach that objective. You identify a service, product, or skill you will develop which will "pay off." Then you must usually work much harder than anyone else even to have a chance at reaching your objective.

Wishing you were rich is merely daydreaming, which is OK as long as you understand what it is and don't get depressed because it doesn't happen.

The more ambitious your money income goal, the more difficult it will probably be for you to reach it. You should be very careful to really think about what it is you really want out of life before you select your money income goal. Many people have spent a lifetime driving themselves to become rich, only to become rich and discover it wasn't really what they wanted after all.

Your money income plan will determine how you will be spending your life, so be careful you set up your plan so that you enjoy what you will be doing.

Rethink the real benefits of where you are right now before you change your direction to a new area of activity. Make this process fun. It's your life and you have enormous opportunity for adventure as long as you are willing to take the risks that go along with continued personal growth.

When you have completed your money income plan, you will know whether you are already where you want to be or whether you need to make some major changes in your life to get where you want to go.

3. YOUR MONEY EXPENSE PLANS

Once you have set your money income objective, you can easily determine your money expense plan. You will have to start asking yourself, "Which would I rather do?"

In the real world, we are always selecting options between alternatives. None of us can do everything we want to do in our lives—even Howard Hughes . . . *especially* Howard Hughes. So as you begin to use your money management strategies to successfully put money to work for you, you are going to stop saying to yourself, "I can't do this or that because it costs too much money." Instead, you are going to be saying, "Which would I rather do?"

Your money expense plan depends on where you are right now and what it will *cost* you to increase your income if you decide you want to do so. It may be that you are living exactly the life you want to live and won't have to alter your expenses. However, if you decide you want to switch careers you will probably have to limit your expenses, especially during the period when your income may be reduced while you get your new career going.

Usually, you can't have it both ways. If you are living on a limited salary, you probably can't take trips to Europe every year and at the same time save enough money to buy an apartment house as an investment. So you are going to be continually asking yourself, "Which would I rather do?"

When you have completed your money expense plan, you will see that you either have enough income to cover your expenses or you don't. If you don't, you are going to have to decide how you will cover these expenses.

4. YOUR MONEY DEBT PLANS

Your debt strategy depends on your money income plan. The more ambitious your money income plan, the greater your debt load will be. But whatever your proposed debt plan, it should be based on going into debt for only two reasons:

1. To buy an asset
2. To buy a necessity

Whether you are borrowing $100 or $1,000,000, you should always ask yourself the following four questions before you borrow the money:

1. How much money do I need to borrow?
2. Why do I need the money?
3. How will I pay it back?
4. How much will it cost me to borrow it?

Borrowing money and handling credit is extremely important, and we will cover the details in the next lesson. The important point is to decide how much debt you can or are willing to handle emotionally and prepare yourself for the time when you will actually have to borrow and repay the money.

When you have completed your money debt plan, you will have determined how you will supply the money you will need to achieve the objectives of your money income plan.

5. YOUR MONEY INVESTMENT PLANS

The key to the success of your long-range planning will be how well you select your investments. Investments aren't limited to material possessions. You invest in yourself when you master a new skill, take a night school course, or spend your time increasing your knowledge and awareness of life's opportunities.

Investing wisely is so important we will cover the subject in Lesson 9. Your primary objective in acquiring investments is to raise your income to the point where it supports your life-style without you having to labor to earn it.

Investments free you from money. Investments enable you to become a capitalist. Once you begin to get your capital working for you, you can devote more of your time to doing the things you want to do in your life.

Your investment plan can be as simple or as complex as you desire it to be. The best investment you can ever make is an investment in yourself.

In today's complex world, it is usually necessary to work with a number of other specialists to maintain a portfolio of profitable investments. There is nothing quite so enjoyable as receiving earnings on one of your investments. And once you begin to accumulate more of them, the multiple effect of earnings starts to work for you until you see your estate taking off, often beyond your wildest dreams.

6. YOUR MONEY REWARD PLANS

As you begin to store up surplus money, your opportunities for paying yourself rewards will increase.

This will be the real test of your progress as a successful money manager. Success often brings down more people than failure—if they are not prepared to handle it. The key to rewarding yourself is to use moderation and discretion in choosing which of many increasing opportunities you will reward yourself with. The person who rewards himself with frequent expensive meals runs the risk of getting fat.

So your challenge will be to use your creative powers to generate a list of imaginative and stimulating rewards for yourself and your family. As you generate more surplus money, you may find yourself spending less of it on your rewards. Excess money frees you from self-denial and by carefully rewarding yourself with selective experiences you enjoy, you will reduce the tension that often comes from the frustration of not being able to do the things you would like to do.

The key to successful management of your rewards is to practice moderation and self-control. The more you move directly into the actual experiences you desire, the less you will be thinking about money and the more creative you will become in making things happen. You will find that there are many ways to achieve the same experience. For example, you can visit San Francisco and stay in the most expensive hotel in town. Or you can select a moderate motel and dine out at the expensive hotel thereby saving money which can be used for other things.

One person always wanted to take an oceangoing cruise. She had six children and never had the money to do so. She also loved handcrafts and developed numerous skills in this area. She used her imagination to land a job teaching handcrafts during the mornings on a cruise ship and was able to take her husband on a four-week cruise. It cost her nothing, as her cabin and meals were paid for by the shipping line in return for her work.

Rewarding yourself is what it's all about. Enjoy giving yourself, your family, and your friends rewards. Relax. Have fun.

SUMMARY

By monitoring these six areas of your life you can become, with practice, a skilled money manager. Since the majority of Americans don't even take time to learn this much about money management, you can become a better money manager by default.

This doesn't mean it's better for people to be uninformed. To the contrary, the better money managers citizens become, the stronger the whole economy becomes and the better it is for all of us.

Keep reminding yourself that money management is a *process.* It's a process you learn by practicing it. You are not searching for some secret out there that will one day enlighten you and turn you into the world's greatest money manager overnight.

What you are doing is practicing with money. You are learning a process just like you learned to cook or to ride a bicycle. The more time you spend practicing, the better you will become.

It is *you* who are raising your own awareness about the reality that surrounds you. As you become more aware, you begin to see more opportunities. As you see more opportunities, you begin to take more risks and lose the fears that come from starting out into the unknown. As the unknown becomes known, you free yourself from emotional and intellectual attitudes toward money which have been holding you back.

This is the basic learning process which you can apply to every part of your life. As you learn, you grow. As you grow, you continue to be aware of the benefits of each stage of your life. It's a wonderful way to live, and it's a living strategy that turns an ordinary life into an exciting one, whoever and wherever you are.

THE REAL VALUE OF PLANNING

Many people get caught up in the paperwork of planning and forget that the principal objective of planning is to give you *thinking* time. What you are doing while you are planning is taking time to step back out of the action and take a focused look at what you are doing and where you are heading.

This is the value of planning! It is not the actual plans themselves; they represent only the *result* of your thinking. So you want to be very careful to keep your plans confidential and to keep your own counsel. There is nothing more discouraging than to have your plans shattered by someone close to you who laughs at your plans when you tell him or her your objective.

Just as you learned to step back and relax during the reprogramming process, you are going to want to take time to plan the direction of your life from now on. If that's too much trouble for you or if you decide you don't want to take the time to plan, that's OK too. This strategy becomes your plan: You plan not to plan.

But should your life ever get out of control or become unsatisfying, you can always regain control by developing written plans for your future.

Planning is a powerful skill you can use to get what you want out of your life and it costs nothing to learn this skill.

YOU DON'T HAVE TO KNOW ALL THE ANSWERS

Many times during your planning, you may find you really don't know what to do. You don't know in which direction to go or what decision to make. That's fine! Be patient. There is no way our conscious brain can think up the right answers to all the questions that come into our lives.

What you are doing when you plan is searching for a way into your internal computer in order to tap the enormous resources we all have available to us once we learn how to relax and listen to our inner voice. The sum of all the experiences we have had is stored in our internal computer, and with the correct strategy most of us can learn to use this resource bank to develop plans for achieving our objectives.

RELAX AND ENJOY IT

So slow down and enjoy the ride. The more tense you get, the more uptight you are and the less chance you will have of reaching your maximum potential. If you are nervous and tense, practice the relaxation techniques suggested in this program until you are able to calm yourself.

At the bottom line of everything we do in life is our individual search for *pleasure.* Keep this in mind while you are developing your plans. A very good rule to remember is: "If it feels good and I like it, it's probably good for me."

This means that if you are into something that generates good vibrations, or something you have really good feelings about, you are probably on the right track. Each of us has an instinctive compass which guides us through life, and we have a much better chance of getting what we want from life if we take time to learn how to read our own compass.

Since each of us is unique, no one else can ever really take over the job of running our life for us. Each of us has to learn to do it ourselves. It was said over a thousand years ago: "Know thyself."

That is the bottom line reason for planning—to know and understand who you are.

So enjoy your planning and be careful to continually review your plans to see whether your plans are supporting you or you are supporting your plans. When you find yourself no longer interested in supporting your plans, *change them!*

DO NOT GO ON TO LESSON 8 UNTIL TOMORROW.

LESSON 8

USING CREDIT TO YOUR OWN ADVANTAGE

> **If you want time to pass quickly, just give a banker your note for 90 days.**
>
> **—R. B. Thomas**

By now, you should agree that until you have got your own "act" together, learning about investments, borrowing, interest payments, tax shelters and so on isn't really very valuable to you. Information becomes valuable to you only when you have a need for it, a reason to use it. You are now ready for that information, and it will be basic common sense.

After you have got your plan worked up, you are going to have to make an important decision as to how you are going to use credit. Credit is nothing more than a term for borrowing. Borrowing is nothing more than a term for using someone else's money instead of your own.

There are people who have borrowed millions of dollars and there are people who have borrowed $5. It is the nature of lenders (people whose money you have borrowed) to want to be *repaid.*

Contrary to public opinion today, you do not have to worry about building up a "credit rating" if you don't want to. You have complete freedom never to borrow a nickel if you so choose. However, for most of us credit is a resource we must use, because we simply do not have the cash available to buy a house or a new car, etc.

Most Americans are extremely poor borrowers. For this reason most American banks and corporations selling products to American people are extremely profitable.

So you will probably have to learn how to use credit successfully. In this lesson you will learn what credit is and how to *put it to work for you.* It won't require any mathematical skills at all (you don't even have to know how to add or subtract).

You will learn how to borrow . . . when to borrow . . . how not to borrow . . . what to borrow money for . . . how to avoid credit traps . . . how to use your banker . . . and many other tips for building sound credit for yourself and your family. Learning this powerful skill will enable you to control your money on your terms so that you can spend it on the things you want.

THE COMPANY STORE

Credit is probably the most misunderstood aspect of money. It is not until you really understand how to use credit that you can become a truly successful money manager.

Credit can stretch your buying power and eventually be used to substantially increase your income-earning potential. But it requires practice and skill to master the use of credit and to end the "credit myths" which have kept many a family in perpetual debt.

A hundred years ago, the "company store" was used to compensate for paying higher wages after slavery was abolished. Wage earners were forced to buy goods at the company store. The company made sure that whatever was paid out in wages came back (and then some) through "credit" extended by the company store. Eventually most wage earners got so deeply in debt there was no way they could bargain for an increase in wages or walk away from their jobs.

The company store was pure and simple robbery. Yet today, a majority of Americans are being milked by the company store concept, except that it has been extended to the whole economy and repackaged as a "credit card."

Every time you use credit to purchase a luxury item, you might as well take dollar bills out of your pocket and toss them into the wind. Every time you use credit to buy something you can afford but that you don't really need (a color TV, a second car, a camper, a trip to Hawaii, a set of golf clubs) you throw away your money no less than if you were to put it in an envelope, tie a rock around it, and throw it into the sea.

Money management is learning how to use credit—learning how to put money to work for you. Before you can hope to increase your capital, you've got to get your credit under control.

DOES THIS MEAN I CAN'T BUY ANYTHING? HAVE FUN? TAKE VACATIONS?

Absolutely not. It means get yourself free of the company store and buy things on your terms, not the 16% to 18% you are going to pay your credit card company for using their expensive little piece of plastic.

Look at it this way. Your cash flow is like a river. Once you get it flowing in your direction, it works for you. You find it easier to enjoy your life and use your judgment to buy the things you need along the way. Once you start getting money to pay you a little extra each month, you begin to accumulate it. Suddenly, you are on top of your expenses.

On the other hand, if you are constantly borrowing more and increasing your debt, your cash flow is working against you. Interest payments get larger. The amount of money you have left over to spend gets smaller and the pressures increase.

Your major credit objective is to get on top of your expenses. You want to build up your credit so that you can use it to increase your capital account.

GETTING OUT OF LOSING GAMES

Remember earlier we talked about all the games that are going on out there to get you to part with your money? You've got to be aware of those games so you can avoid them. The stakes are high. For example, there are at least 85 million adult Americans around spending their money every day. If a company can get each of us to part with only $1 a year, their sales will be $85 million. Not bad for a year's work. If the product they are selling you costs them $0.20 to make, they will have $68 million to spend. Let's say they want to keep $10 million for themselves. That leaves $58 million they can spend to get you to give them your dollar.

That buys a lot of newspaper, magazine, and TV ads. For only $5,200,000 they can run an ad once a week all year long on network TV. What chance have you got?

If you are aware of what's going on, you have a great chance to get out of their game. Once you understand why it is you suddenly get an irresistible urge to buy the new $1-grapefruit peeler and you know someone has spent 58 million of their dollars to give you this "need," you will get a lot of satisfaction laughing your way to the bank with your $1. Let someone else get hooked into buying something they don't really need.

Every minute of every day someone is out there spending their money to make you think you need their product. The majority of the things you think you need have been programmed into your head. You are being motivated to buy things. Social pressure is constantly being put on you to spend your money.

When the majority of your needs are filled, people come along and invent new needs. Just when you are finally paying off all your old credit card purchases . . . bang . . . there it is on the old TV—something new you've just got to have! After everyone has bought all the cars they can possibly park in their driveway, someone comes along and "invents" the CB radio and there goes another $150 on the credit card.

Your most important money management job is to wake up and shake yourself out of the hypnotic state into which you are lulled every day by ads communicated to you through TV, radio, newspaper, magazine, and cereal box. You've got to be sure you are buying what you want, not what someone else wants you to buy.

This doesn't mean you can't fill your house with all the latest electronic gadgets on the market. You can. It's your money—your life. But you want to be sure it's what you really want and not something you've been programmed to buy. Make a direct, conscious choice; let it stand the test of direct, open scrutiny from your planning system.

GETTING FREE

Now most money management programs get into credit management without ever covering this base. But by now you should see that credit begins with your ability to control your spending. The beginning of managing credit is an *emotional* experience, not a financial technique.

Most of us become addicted to spending money on what we are programmed to buy. We become suckers who hand out our money to anybody with a good, convincing advertisement. Unless we can get over our addictions, we won't be able to handle credit successfully.

Look at this another way. Consider a person who smokes a pack and a half of cigarettes a day and drinks a six-pack of beer every two days. Moreover, this person trades in his car every year and plays golf every Saturday. This person complains that taxes are too high to save any money. But the truth is that this person is supporting a $2,000-a-year habit.

To get free of the "money games" other people are trying to get you to play, you are going to have to reprogram your attitudes so that you know you have control over the flow of your money.

When you have accomplished this, you are ready to explore the world of credit and see how you can use it successfully. Just as it does little good for a person to buy a pair of ice skates if there is never any ice around to skate on, it doesn't do a person much good to know all the "rules" of credit if he or she hasn't got a strategy for controlling expenses. Money management is learning how to control the flow of your money. You do this by controlling your thinking and behavior patterns and by controlling the influence other people have over you. Once you are in control, you are free of the power money can have over you and you are ready to use your control to develop successful credit strategies.

CREDIT—WHAT IT'S REALLY ALL ABOUT

The principal objective of credit is to provide "liquidity" to the economy. Credit frees buying power from "frozen" assets. Credit is not there to be used to buy things you can't afford.

For example, let's say you have lived in your house for ten years. During that time you have reduced your mortgage to $15,000. Your house will now bring $30,000 on the market. Therefore, you now have $15,000 "frozen" into your house. Without credit the only way you could get this money would be to sell your house. But then where would you live? So you go to your banker and arrange to borrow against the value of your house. Since the banker is renting you money, he or she will most likely lend you 80% of the value of your house. The extra 20% is kept in reserve in case the market goes down or other costs are necessary in selling the house. You can then borrow a total of $24,000 against the "security" of your house. Since your mortgage is $15,000, you can now borrow an additional $9,000.

Sometimes the security for your credit is your car. Sometimes it is your job. Sometimes it is your good record and reputation.

Credit is created when someone else digs into his or her pocket to give you something (money, a product, a service) which you can't or do not want to pay for with your money. The motivation for their generosity is *profit.* By extending you credit, they end up getting money out of your pocket. They charge you interest. Instead of paying $350 for your TV, you pay $425 and the lenders pocket the extra $75. Instead of paying $3,500 for your car, you pay $4,800 and they pocket the extra $1,300. Instead of paying $28,000 for your house, you pay $44,000 and they pocket the extra $16,000. The point is that every time you use your credit, you pay for it. Is this OK with you? Be aware that's what you are agreeing to do.

THE BIG MISUNDERSTANDING

For some reason, when the great credit card bonanza hit the market, most people failed to really understand its implications. Instead of putting money away and saving for a new car or TV or dishwasher, everyone started buying these things on credit. Instead of putting away $100 every month into your bank and being *paid* interest on it, people started buying things on credit and ended up *paying* the bank each month for their money. This was very profitable for the banks and very unprofitable for us.

There are people right now who are in even a worse position. They keep money in their savings account on which the bank pays them 5% interest and at the same time keep a running balance on the credit card on which the bank charges them 18%. People who do this don't understand credit or don't care.

Usually, just about the time you finally pay off that once new car or dishwasher or TV, you discover that it breaks down or that you've just got to have the newest, latest model. So your friendly supplier gives you a discount, a trade-in for your old model. Big deal! You paid for every inch of it. Suddenly you are right back in the middle of the credit trap—payments every month.

So the first thing you've got to do if you want to use your credit successfully is to get yourself off the 18% treadmill.

HOW CAN I DO THAT?

You can begin today by rethinking your money management strategy, especially as it relates to using credit.

Think, for a moment, of your money as if it were water running through a hose. Assuming that you have a way to earn money each month, imagine that your money is being spent as if you were turning a hose on and off. If you do not manage your money well, at the end of the month, or before the end of the month, the water will suddenly stop running. Your water reserve will be empty. If you do not plan ahead and manage your money, at the end of the month, there will be none left over, no reservoir into which you have run some of that water.

Your primary objective is to start filling that reservoir with water until there is so much of it that it will take care of your needs for the rest of your life without ever running out. The way you do that is by limiting your expenses so that there is a small reserve, or savings, left over which you invest.

We recommend you achieve this by setting up a schedule on which you pay yourself first, pay your bills second, and then put a little into your emergency account. What is left over is what you have to spend on non-essentials for the month.

This strategy will "turn around" your money flow and begin to start you out on the right money path.

Until you have reached this level of skill in managing your money, don't even think about establishing your credit. If you are over your head with bills now and sinking, bite the bullet; cut back your expenses. If you have credit cards, lock them away someplace until you have reversed the money flow in your direction.

THE TWO CREDIT RULES

Other things you might do to get yourself out of a credit trap are to sell some of your assets. Have a garage sale. Take those old college textbooks to a second-hand dealer and see if you can get something for them. The amount you get isn't so important! You are trying to turn around your money flow, and every dollar helps. Think in dollars and cents, and save every dime you can get your hands on until you start to reverse your money flow. You are reversing your thinking little by little this way—nothing is too small a step. It results in attitude changes that free you up.

As soon as you begin to see that your monthly payments are getting less—not more—you are on your way to putting money to work for you. You have taken the first important step toward managing your money to work for you.

Before you unlock your credit cards and put them back in your wallet or purse, study these two credit rules:

USE YOUR CREDIT FOR ONLY TWO REASONS

1. *To acquire an asset:*

   Use credit to buy something that has a long-term value, something you will be able to sell later on. If you won't be able to sell something later on for as much as or more than you paid for it, *it isn't an asset.*

   This means . . . a house, a painting, antique furniture, stamps, coins, a plot of land, stocks, bonds, etc., are assets. It is probable that you can sell these things later on for as much as or more than the purchase price.

   This means . . . your car (unless it is an antique), your clothing, your TV, etc., are not assets. Anything that is not an asset is a *consumable item,* something you use up.

2. *To buy a necessity:*

   A necessity is something you really need—a car, your teeth fixed, a lawn mower. A necessity is something you know you need but usually don't like to spend money on. If you find yourself wanting to spend money on something, chances are it isn't a necessity—something you really need—but a luxury, something you've been programmed to think you need.

That's all there is to mastering the use of credit. Two rules. Use credit only to buy an asset or to buy something which is a necessity.

Credit is most generally misused when either of these two rules is broken. You misuse credit when you use credit to buy non-essential goods.

YOU ARE MISUSING CREDIT WHEN YOU USE CREDIT TO BUY:

1. A dinner out on the town
2. Clothing, shoes
3. Records, tapes, alcohol, groceries
4. Golf clubs, tennis balls
5. Luxury items of any kind

KEY POINT

You are going to have to ask yourself every time you decide to buy something: Which would I rather have?

1. The thing I want to buy?
2. The savings I will have from not buying it?
3. Something else I could buy if I didn't buy the item in question?

BUT HOW CAN I ENJOY LIFE THEN? DO I HAVE TO GIVE UP QUALITY?

Absolutely not. You are simply reversing your money flow. For example, suppose you want to buy a set of new golf clubs for $350. Instead of putting them on the credit card, you save $50 a month for seven months. *Then* you buy the golf clubs. That's one option you have. And you have truly made this happen: You can actually acquire two things—the golf clubs and the real sense of having made it all happen. However, there are many other imaginative ways you can get the same quality by using your ingenuity. Why do you need brand new clubs? Every day there must be someone ready to throw their golf clubs in the water hole and forget the game for life, or someone who wants to switch to tennis, or someone who is just too old to play anymore. Look around and there is a chance you may pick up a set of golf clubs for $100 with the same, or even better, quality than that of a brand new set.

If this happens, you have saved $250 which is not on a credit card and which you are not paying 18% interest on. You may find a new set of golf clubs that sell for $150 which will work just as well for you. In this case you have saved $200.

KEY POINT

> REMEMBER: Every time you *save* money by not buying something or by buying it for less than you might have paid for it, you put money in your pocket and increase your sense of yourself as being able to make things happen in your world—whatever that might be.

It used to be that looking for a "good buy" was a matter of pride. It was called old Yankee ingenuity. Lately, TV ads and other media advertisements have tried to make it look like you are dumb to buy anything but something brand new. The ads make it seem that the most *expensive* item is always the best buy for you. While it is usually true that "you get what you pay for," you may also be able to get what someone else paid for—and for less! This way, you will achieve your personal financial peace of mind by educating yourself as a consumer, practicing conservation, and taking every money-saving buy you can find along the way.

Use your imagination to buy things. Make it a game. And besides, if you can find someone else who wants to sell what you need directly to you, both of you benefit without paying the 18% penalty that credit demands.

Examine your needs and your standard of quality. If you are always hurting at the end of the month, maybe you are looking for a quality you can't really afford. If you are into $300 or $500 suits, maybe you can find a $150 suit which will do just as well. A solid gold pen looks nice, but it only takes a $0.50 pen to write with. Both do the same job. Look to the reason you want to buy something and make sure you aren't being programmed into overspending. A $5,000 bargain on a new Rolls Royce isn't a saving if you can really only afford a $3,000 Honda. So don't spend yourself poor buying "bargains" that aren't.

BUYING TIP

Unless you are buying an asset or something you've planned and saved for, never spend more than you make in a day.

This little technique will automatically keep you out of a lot of trouble. For example, if your take-home pay is $1,200 a month and you pay yourself $150 each month and put away $50 each month for vacation and $50 for emergencies, that means what you have left over is $950 a month. Divide that by 30 days and you make $31.66 each day. Unless you are buying something you've planned for, limit your purchases to $32 in one day.

CREDIT TIP

Use "teacup" economics to control your spending habits.

The 10-step money management system in Lesson 4 is based on the strategy of teacup economics. First you pay yourself, then you pay your bills, then you put away money for emergencies, vacations, etc. What is left over is what you can spend. If nothing is left over, you have nothing to spend. Use this approach to your spending. This way you will constantly be increasing your assets. You will always have some money to spend and can have fun and won't go begging. You will be slowly increasing your net worth and your estate and in a shorter period than you think, you will be looking around for investments.

DO NOT GO ON TO LESSON 9 UNTIL TOMORROW.

LESSON 9

INVESTING SUCCESSFULLY

> **There are two times in your life when you should not speculate . . . when you can't afford it, and when you can.**
>
> **—Mark Twain**

Mark Twain knew what he was talking about. After years of the life of a successful writer and speaker, he lost most of the money he had earned on several lunatic investments doomed to fail from the beginning. Jack London lost a small fortune investing in eucalyptus trees.

Every hour of every day, people who have spent a lifetime making and saving money lose it, because they do not understand the first thing about investing it.

Investing money is one of the few games in which the player who knows what he is doing *prefers* to play with people who do not. In other games—bridge, chess, tennis—people seek out opponents who are equal to them in skill. Not true with the money game! Though it might be boring to play one of those other games day after day with an opponent so bad there wasn't even a challenge, the sophisticated investor loves nothing more than to collect money twenty-four hours a day from people dumb enough to hand it over. Somehow the continued profits make the game worth playing.

ARE YOU A SOPHISTICATED INVESTOR?

There is no mystery about it and deep in your heart you know the answer. I'll bet I know the answer! But that's OK, because the best thing in your life is to admit you don't know a damn thing about investing your money. Taking that step alone will keep you out of 80% of the bad investments you might otherwise make.

Just as you learned the sound principles of using credit, you can learn the sound principles of investing your money. If you continue to follow the techniques of this 9-day money management program, you are going to eventually begin to accumulate surplus money. If you want to beat inflation, you are going to want to invest that money wisely. You are going to want to "cross over" to the other side of the money transaction and become the lender rather than the borrower, the investor rather than the buyer, the owner rather the renter.

Investing requires more planning and attention than making money. It is here that most people go wrong. After years of hard work earning surplus money, they suddenly lose it in bad investments. Well, you don't have to worry about that, because this lesson will show you how to become a sophisticated investor who can confidently invest money into opportunities that work for you.

Many other people miss these "real" investment opportunities, because they are still afraid of money and think they can simply turn it over to someone else to invest for them. People who are still afraid of money make very bad investors indeed.

This lesson will show you how to take risks successfully . . . how to avoid losing money . . . the best investment you can make . . . and how to protect the money you already have. You will learn how to invest your money with confidence . . . how to control your investments to your advantage . . . and how to avoid the investment traps that cause other people to take substantial losses.

More important, you will learn how to start avoiding the investments that really don't pay off for you anymore—the kind of "safe" investments that in truth are not investments at all but simply ways of letting someone else use your money to make money for themselves.

After mastering the techniques in this lesson, you will minimize your fear of investing money: You will find it fun and exciting and profitable. You will always have a way to use extra money and place it in investments that pay off for you in more ways than one.

GETTING RICH THE SLOW WAY

If you start following the money management strategies in this program, one day you will experience the beautiful reality of becoming a capitalist in its most wonderful and exciting sense. One day, you are going to look over your financial situation and you will discover something.

You will be salting away money every month. You will have reserved enough for emergencies and vacations. Your cash account will be up to 50% of your annual take-home pay. And there it will be—*something left over!* There will be a sum of money you can afford to invest in something that will pay you more than the 5% interest you can get from your local bank or savings and loan association.

BE CAREFUL!

Oddly enough, it is at this point in your financial career that you stand to win or lose a lot in your money game. The initial struggle to accumulate money can take a long time. Often you are not prepared psychologically or technically to handle the "high" that comes from finally making it—from finally being a capitalist.

At this point many people lose the money game by using the wrong investment strategy. Because all their skills have been developed learning how to save and conserve money, they really haven't mastered the skills of *investing* money. The two greatest mistakes people make at this time are:

1. INVESTING IN A GET-RICH-QUICK SCHEME
2. TRYING TO GET SOMETHING FOR NOTHING

If you can avoid both these investment traps, you have a very good chance of really making some money over the coming years.

AN INTELLIGENT INVESTMENT STRATEGY

Your investment strategy should be an extension of your existing money management strategy. In other words, you should invest in yourself . . . in something you know about . . . and in an amount that protects your existing capital and limits your risks.

A lot of people think that investing money is an easy trip —just sitting around clipping coupons. It may have been true years ago, but today, with inflation and other complications in our society, investing money requires even more energy than earning money and managing it.

We suggest that you continue to follow the money management process that this program outlines. It requires patience and common sense and an interest in what you are doing, thinking, and feeling. We can't guarantee that you will end up a millionaire, but we can guarantee that you will have an excellent chance of continuing to increase your net worth, of enjoying the opportunities capital brings, and of finding out where you want to be in the financial system.

The difference between just managing your income and managing your income and your capital is that you are now building a second story on your house of money. The same techniques apply to investing money that apply to earning and spending it.

The greatest mistake most people make is that they try to hurry the process. An intelligent money management strategy recognizes that it takes time to build an estate. Just as the farmer must plant the seed and then wait until nature turns it into a crop, the intelligent money manager must wait patiently until the "investment seed" returns long-term profits. When you try to hurry the process or to get rich quick, you usually kill the investment before it can grow into profit.

YOU MEAN THERE IS NO WAY I CAN GET RICH QUICK?

That's right.

Unless you are simply gambling your money away, there will be little chance for you to get rich quick. The stories you hear about stocks shooting up and oil wells paying off and real estate skyrocketing are the exceptions not the rules. Get-rich-quick schemes generally make a high, steady income for the promoters and big losses for the investors.

SO WHAT CAN I DO?

The first intelligent step is not to start your investment program until you have taken care of your basic needs. For many families it takes years before they reach the capitalist stage, if at all. Before you begin to seriously look at any investments other than a home, a savings account, antique furniture, or any other thing you need or want around the house, you should at least have taken care of the following basic money management necessities:

1. Insurance policies to cover emergencies, death, accidents, disability, etc.
2. Cash in savings accounts equal to at least 50% of your take-home pay for one year (i.e., six months).
3. Cash in savings accounts to cover emergencies, vacations, etc.
4. Down payment for your home, condominium, etc.
5. Regular savings set up for your retirement account.

Only after these essentials have been taken care of should you seriously be looking at outside investments.

WHY?

Because an investor has to be someone who can afford to lose whatever he or she puts into an investment and someone who can sit back and wait for the investment to grow —someone who is financially and emotionally willing to risk a loss.

Until you have taken care of your financial necessities, you cannot have those two resources available to you. Moreover, your best investment is your home. Buying a home or a condominium or whatever usually pays off handsomely over the years and in most cases is the *only* investment many people end up with after a lifetime of work. There simply isn't anything you can invest in during your working years that has the chance of paying off as well as your home.

Whenever you can invest in something you need, you get a double benefit—the use of it and the appreciation on your investment. In other words, you are investing in yourself!

KEY POINT

> We recommend an investment strategy of investing in yourself whenever the opportunity arises.

This means deciding what it is you love to do and increasing your skills in doing it. For example, suppose you love to paint houses. There are a lot more people around that don't like to paint houses. A small investment in setting up your own house painting company can pay off handsomely for you.

Suppose you love to play golf. Finding a way to invest in golf (repping for a golf ball company, designing and marketing a golfing hat, buying the franchise for soft drinks at your local club, whatever) can pay off handsomely for you.

Whenever you can put your money into something you enjoy doing, you are well ahead of the person desperately looking around for someone to help him or her invest his or her money.

A COMMON SENSE INVESTMENT PROGRAM

Adhere to the following investment rules and you will be as good an investor as anyone in your generation:

1. BUY LOW, SELL HIGH

Whatever you get into, you must plan to sell whatever it is for more than you paid for it. If you don't, what reason is there to put your money into it?

2. BECOME AN EXPERT IN WHATEVER IT IS YOU INVEST IN

Now who is going to have a better chance of making a profitable investment: someone who knows the investment inside and out, who understands the marketplace, and who has tracked similar investments, or someone who hands money to someone else and says, "Here, take my money and invest it for me"?

It doesn't cost money to become an expert. Most information is only a phone call away or a trip to your local library—and it's fun to become an expert.

If you want to get into the stock market—great! A year or so before you are ready to invest, start learning everything you can about the stock market. Read books. Ask questions. Invest your time and extra spending money in your new interest.

Six months before you decide to invest, give yourself $1,000,000! That's right. Give yourself $1,000,000 or $10,000,000 on paper and start making investments in the stock market. Keep your records for six months and then add up where you are. Did you come out ahead or behind? How much did your investing pay off? What did you learn? What do you still need to know?

3. LET THE OTHER PERSON TAKE THE RISK

If you are going into a more complicated business, start out small and let the other person take the risk. Become a small, limited partner. Suppose you want to buy real estate, fix it up and sell it for a higher price. Look around for someone who is already doing it successfully. Put together a group of people to make the first purchase. Pool your resources and limit your risks. Don't put all your money into an investment while you are still an amateur. Become a *pro.* When you become a pro, your chances for making a profit will skyrocket.

4. INVESTING IS FUN

Enjoy investing your money! If you follow these investment principles, you will automatically find many opportunities for personal rewards opening up for you. Be careful not to be pressured into an investment by someone in your family or one of your friends. Keep your own counsel. Limit your risks and cut your losses quickly.

5. DON'T BE PRESSURED

The investment of a lifetime often turns out to be just that but for different reasons. Usually, it's the investment of a lifetime because in a few weeks or months it is bankrupt. When somebody comes to you with a sure-fire investment that requires you to invest today before it slips out of your reach, learn to "reach" very slowly. The seasoned investor knows that there are always good investments out there and that there is no need for hurrying into one investment.

True, once in a million times a person does get a chance to buy a gold mine for a few dollars or an oil lease for less, which becomes the bonanza investment of all time. Some people also win the Irish Sweepstakes. But an investment program based on winning the Irish Sweepstakes or the Kentucky Derby is doomed to failure.

Make the investments you want to make. You are mastering a process. You will become a successful investor when you master money and your judgment becomes professional. So don't worry about the missed opportunities along the way. There are a hundred times more missed disasters along the path to profitable investing than missed opportunities.

6. DON'T CONFUSE GAMBLING WITH INVESTING

Maybe you want to gamble with some of your money. Fine. Great. Good luck. But don't confuse gambling with investing. When you invest, you are taking a calculated risk based on your experience that the investment will pay off, because a service or product has a market. The odds are in your favor.

When you gamble (unless you own the casino), the odds are *always against you.* Gambling is a form of entertainment. It has nothing to do with investing.

7. USE THE SPECIALISTS AND PAY YOUR MONEY FOR THE BEST

Don't become an amateur investor. The amateur investor always trys to do everything himself. The amateur investor does not pay for special information.

Your best investment is people who are specialists in their field. Find the best and pay what they charge. Get the best banker, the best attorney, the best broker, the best CPA. You are buying their experience—not to invest for you but to evaluate your investment strategy. The money you pay them is fully deductible. It is the best investment you can make.

8. START SMALL

Conrad Hilton started out by buying a run-down, little old hotel somewhere in nowhere, Texas. He learned the hotel business and then built hotels all around the world. Walk before you run.

You learn just as much from a small investment as a big one. If you want to go into the antique business, spend a few years buying things for your house and then prove that you can sell them for more than you paid for them. After this you may be ready to open your own shop.

Be sure you are protected when you invest as a partner. Limit your investment. If you lose it that's OK. Learn why it didn't work.

9. DON'T CHASE A LOSING INVESTMENT

Your best friend comes to you and says it will only take $1,000 to make a million. So you invest in his or her new "invention." Six months later he or she comes back and says it will only take another $500 to hit the jackpot.

Be nice, polite, and firm in your "No, thank you." A small investor simply can't afford to chase a losing investment. You have no moral obligation to invest any more than when you agreed to invest the first time around. Don't be pressured into adding your hard-earned dollars into a down-sliding investment.

10. BUY YOUR INVESTMENT MONEY AS CHEAPLY AS YOU CAN

After you really get moving and find you are making good investments, it won't take you long to discover the first rule of money, which is that large amounts of money earn more than small amounts.

When you know what you are doing and your investments are paying off you will say, "Wow, if I only had $1,000,000 to invest instead of $5,000, I'd really clean up." Now you are getting ready to consider larger investments.

You have established your credit and learned your business. Instead of investing in a duplex you want to invest in a 100-room hotel. Fine. Great. Why not?

There comes a point when you are going to be buying or renting money. You are going to be looking for an ROI, or rate of *return on investment.* At this point investing becomes bookkeeping. You are going to begin to invest larger and larger amounts of money, much more than you could ever hope to earn or squeeze out of your existing assets. You are now looking at the professional use of credit.

Once you accumulate sufficient capital to be expanding your investments in this way, your profit will be the difference between what you pay for money and what you get back as profit.

If you can borrow $100 from your bank for one year and pay 9.5% interest, it will cost you $9.50 to borrow that money for a year. If you can—after paying all costs—invest that $100 in something that will pay you 15%, at the end of the year you will have made $15.00, spent $9.50, and earned a profit of $5.50.

That's what it's all about—big-time investment. That's what all those expensive computers and busy business school graduates and high-priced attorneys are doing all day long—figuring how to rent money so that a profit results.

It may not sound too exciting at $100 a year, but figure out what 5.5% of $10,000,000 is: $550,000 in income ought to pay for most of your luxury items.

WHO, ME? BORROW $10,000,000?

Why not? When you know what you are doing and you are ready, you will find all kinds of people out there dying to give it to you. That's the next big secret about borrowing money.

It's hard as hell to get $15,000 on your signature alone, but go after $10,000,000 and people will hand it over to you. As long as they are convinced that you really know what you are doing.

There's a reason for this. The larger the amount of money, the more difficult it is for a person—borrower or lender alike—to imagine what it means. Just about everyone can handle, say, $5,000 or $10,000, because we can drive our $5,000 car to work and spend the weekend in our $10,000 camper. But $10,000,000! It takes a lot of imagination to "picture" that.

So people who get paid to invest large sums of money aren't looking at money. They are looking at collateral. In other words, what is it they are trading their cash for? You would probably have a lot of trouble convincing someone to hand over $15,000 of their money on your word you would give them $20,000 back in five years. But you won't have any trouble getting them to hand over $5,000,000 if they will be investing in a building worth $10,000,000. They can "see" where their money is.

You may never get to the point where you want to borrow a large sum of money, but the same principle applies whether it is $15 or $15,000,000. You will find it easy to borrow money if you have collateral and difficult to borrow if you don't.

SUMMARY

Investing money is an acquired skill which takes time, experience, and courage. The amount the investment returns usually depends upon the risk. High-risk investments return higher profits when they succeed. Low-risk investments (savings accounts, etc.) return lower profits.

There is no magic investment program, no secret investment principle, no 5-step investment program to make you rich. There can't be such a program because the major cause of your success as an investor is *you.* Unless you can develop the necessary skills to become an investor, you won't succeed.

THE INVESTMENT IS YOURSELF

That's it. Enjoy your life and find out what turns you on. Then use your capital to slowly invest in something you know something about. Cut your losses quickly and ride your winners and you've got an excellent opportunity to live a rewarding life with plenty left over at the other end of it.

You are your best investment. By learning skills and by developing your own resources, you become "valuable" to the community. You have something to give. Once you have something to give, you have created a market. Once you have created a market, you have developed a way to earn money. That's what investing is all about.

THE MORE YOU GIVE, THE MORE YOU GET.

PUTTING IT ALL TOGETHER

Here's to you, as good as you
are,
May you live all the days of
your life.
—Swift

For years I suffered because I was looking for the *secrets* of life. I went around believing other people knew something I didn't know or knew more than I knew. I believed one day someone would take time to let me in on the game.

Eventually, I became aware that most of these other people were in the same boat I was in. Each of them was wandering around looking for someone to let them in on the secrets of the game of life too. True, some of these people seemed to be secure. They had developed money management strategies or had inherited so much money that it was no longer a problem in their lives. But as I began to increase my circle of friends and acquaintances, I noticed that these so-called financially secure people often had enormous problems in other areas of their lives.

Then I noticed another group of people—people who seemed to have gotten it all together, who appeared to be genuinely at peace and at harmony with their world. A common thread ran through this group of people. They were all *enjoying* their lives. They accepted life with its ups and downs and lived for each day. They spent their lives doing things they enjoyed.

THERE ARE NO SECRETS

If life were constant so that each of us were born into a world that never changed, there *would be* important social secrets each of us could learn to make our way better through life. There have been times in the past when societies have been stable for several hundred years. But even so, the real joy of life usually comes from discovering the excitement of the self—of being free to explore the unknown of life and to grow without restriction.

In our highly technological society, things are changing so quickly it is vital for us to develop an inner strength—an *energy resource* which can be used to survive successfully on our own terms and to control technology rather than have it control us.

The process through which each of us can do this is *awareness.* This word "aware" has gotten a big play recently and has become one of the buzz words we hear people saying all around us. What it really means is that we have turned ourselves on to life rather than continued to move through life with blinders on. It is by becoming aware of our potential that we expand our universe.

It is really up to each of us to *create* the kind of life we want to live. With all the billions of people on earth, each of us is uniquely different. The world works because each of us has different goals, interests, and skills.

The sad thing is that so many of us overlook our potential, because we have not become aware of all the opportunities around us. So many of us miss the chance to live life on our own terms simply because we haven't opened our eyes.

There is a story about a pet parrot who was tied by his leg to his perch. Every time he tried to fly away, he failed. After a while the parrot never tried to fly again. The parrot was untied from the perch but stayed there for the rest of his life. Though perfectly able to fly, the parrot had reprogrammed himself not to fly. The parrot was no longer aware he had the ability to fly.

YOUR ATTITUDES CREATE YOUR GAME

In this program we have tried to take a new approach to money management. We have tried to put you in the driver's seat of your own life. We have tried to help you become *aware* of the process of managing money.

If we have succeeded, you will probably have a whole new attitude toward money now. This will be true because you will have a whole new attitude toward yourself. If you have become aware of the millionaire's attitude toward money, you will now realize the enormous potential you have to control your own financial future on your own terms. You will understand why the poverty attitude shuts off opportunity and limits your future. You will see that you are not isolated, alone, and battling against the rest of the world but the person who set up the games you are playing now.

Your first step to financial independence is to select money attitudes that work for you. Once you have selected the appropriate attitudes, you can then begin to use the technical skills of money management to make things happen your way. The important thing to remember is that you are the one who is *learning* a new skill. If you aren't getting anywhere, if you find yourself falling down, you probably haven't learned how to play the game yet. Don't get discouraged. PRACTICE! Fail successfully!

MAKING A LOT OF MONEY IS HARD WORK

You **can make** a million dollars. People do it every day, but be prepared to work for it. Becoming wealthy is like gaining weight: You don't go from 167 pounds to 350 pounds overnight. It takes months, sometimes years of overeating to put on those extra pounds. The same thing is usually true of making a fortune. It takes dedicated, consistent, hard work. But if that's what you want to do and you enjoy working—why not?

Fortunately, for most of us our capitalistic system works very well. It does not take an enormous amount of money to enjoy life. As a middle-income earner, we can generally expect to go through life with excellent opportunities for self-satisfaction and continued rewards. The money management techniques you have learned in this program can stretch your income so that you have a better chance of getting the things you want out of your life along the way.

Managing your money (along with your other resources) can give you an element of control over your life you otherwise might not have. It can be the difference between just drifting through life and making things happen your way.

KNOW YOURSELF

Essentially, we come back to the fact that you are creating your life each day—directing it along its path. Once you become aware of this, you can begin to take control of (i.e., manage) your life's script. That's usually when life starts to become fun. Once you become aware that you are not trapped into what you are doing but are doing it because *you* have placed yourself where you are, you can begin to see how you can move out of your present situation and into another one.

In the end, we do battle only with ourselves. Once we understand this and focus our energy on what we can do to control our own lives (and not what other people can do to us) we begin to gain important insights into how life works. So you can pretty well tell where you are in a particular skill area by where your attention is focused. Beginners and amateurs tend to worry a lot about what other people—mostly their opponents—can do to them. Professionals develop an awareness of their own strengths and weaknesses and concentrate on getting their own game in shape.

ELIMINATING THE TRAPS OF SUCCESS

Hopefully, as you begin to succeed as a money manager, you are going to gain in confidence. You will be at your most vulnerable point after you have achieved your immediate objectives and feel the power and excitement of finally knowing that you have gained control over this part of your life. BE CAREFUL!

It is always a good strategy not to let success go to your head or bend your behavior. Keep focused on your real objectives and continue to question your activities even though you may be riding a streak of winning situations. Try not to become OVERCONFIDENT.

By sticking to your plans, you can avoid a lot of the pitfalls that success sometimes brings.

THE FINAL CHALLENGE

If you have followed this program and understand its fundamental principles, you will now have a series of techniques you can use to discard what doesn't work for you and replace it with something that does work. And you will realize that your worth to everyone else depends on what you can do that works for *them.* When you have developed a skill, a service, or a product that works for other people, you have established a means of generating income. The more you can give, the more you will get in return.

Each of us has a unique mix of strengths and weaknesses which we can use to reach our maximum level of potential. By developing a strategy to manage our money, we can improve our chances for establishing the kind of economic base most of us need to support our lives.

This program is a beginning. You are going to have to develop your own money management strategy—the one that works for you, your family, your friends, and your fellow workers. This process can be exciting and enjoyable and, most important, profitable.

You are the world's greatest expert on yourself. You know more about yourself than anyone else will ever know. You can make things happen your way. By becoming a successful money manager, you can open up new opportunities in your life. Whether or not you take advantage of these opportunities is up to you. Good luck.

QUESTIONS & ANSWERS

WHY DO I ALWAYS SEEM TO BE HAVING MONEY PROBLEMS?

Chances are you haven't learned how to play the money game yet. If you have never played golf, you would probably never consent to play in the Masters tournament. If you have never played bridge, you probably wouldn't sit down at the table with three life master players and play for a dollar a point. If you don't know how to drive a car, you don't take one out on the Hollywood Freeway at five o'clock in the afternoon. Yet most of us go through life playing the money game without knowing what we are doing. No wonder so many of us come up losers. You can easily learn how to play the money game by mastering the techniques contained in this 9-Day Money Management Program.

WHAT CAN I DO ABOUT INFLATION?

Everybody seems to be worrying about inflation. Instead, concentrate on becoming a successful money manager. As long as you provide a service, product, or skill which is valuable to other people, you can count on being able to earn a living. As long as you are willing to work, you don't have to worry. You beat inflation by practicing the sound financial principles contained in this program. If you are retired on a fixed income, you can still manage your money so that you get the most out of it. Beat inflation by controlling your *expenses.*

HOW SHOULD I INVEST MY MONEY?

You should tailor your investments to your specific lifestyle, needs, interests, talents, and goals. Invest in yourself. Find something you love to do and invest step by step in it. Use your imagination. Don't invest in anything you don't thoroughly understand. Pay specialists and experts to advise you before making an investment. Wait until you have at least $6,000 to $10,000 in your permanent savings account before you start thinking about more sophisticated investments. Investing money is a skill you can learn.

HOW CAN I GET OUT OF ALL THESE MONTHLY BILLS?

Assuming that you have an adequate source of income, you can get yourself out of chronic debt by practicing control over your expenses. Lock up your credit cards and charge account cards until you have paid all your outstanding balances off. Use the 10-step Cash Flow Management

System (pages 55–62) to turn the money flow in your direction. Check to see if one or more expensive habits (smoking, excessive drinking, overeating) are draining your money away. Set up a realistic monthly money plan to get the most out of your income.

HOW CAN I AVOID FAMILY ARGUMENTS OVER MONEY?

Often arguments about money aren't really money arguments at all. Money is often used to "test" relationships between family members. By sharing your financial goals and plans, and by regularly discussing your financial situation together, you can develop an objective approach to money management which will meet the needs of each member of your family. Give each family member an opportunity to express his or her money needs, fears, and worries; don't try to anticipate or guess what the other person is feeling. The more financial information a family shares, the less chance there will be arguments over money.

HOW CAN I AVOID PAYING HIGH INCOME TAXES?

Most people worry too much about paying taxes and not enough about managing their money successfully. Find what options you have by paying a professional tax consultant to assist you with your tax preparation and tax planning. Be honest when you prepare your tax returns. Take every legitimate deduction but avoid complicated tax shelters that you do not thoroughly understand. Use forward planning (e.g., retirement funds, life insurance) to develop a long-range investment program that will give you the best tax advantages over the years. Enjoy paying high taxes. It means you are earning more money than the average person. With careful money management you can stretch your income to get the things you want out of life without worrying excessively about taxes.

HOW CAN I GET RICH QUICK?

You can't. You may get lucky and win a lottery or the Irish Sweepstakes, but there is no legitimate and realistic way to get rich quick. Wealth is the accumulation of surplus resources you receive because you are providing a service, product, or skill to someone else. It takes time, persistence, and hard work to develop something to sell that will result in wealth for you. Concentrate instead on the things you love to do in life. Learn how to do them as best you can. Enjoy the rewards of doing them, and one day you, like thousands of other Americans, may discover that you have become wealthy.

HOW CAN I KEEP FROM LOSING THE MONEY I ALREADY HAVE?

Keep away from investments that offer you "something for nothing" or the chance to "strike it rich," and carefully invest your money in things that you thoroughly understand. If you do go into a risky investment area, take time to learn as much as you can about that *investment game* before you put your money into it. Resist those investments that are being sold to you as the "chance of a lifetime." You accumulate wealth over the long term by becoming skilled as an investor, not because you hit on a lucky opportunity once in your life. Pay specialists with unquestioned integrity to advise you, but don't automatically follow their advice, and do not invest if you do not thoroughly understand what it is you are investing in.

IS IT TOO LATE FOR ME TO BECOME A SUCCESSFUL MONEY MANAGER?

No matter where you are starting from, you can improve your skills as a money manager. The less income you have, the more important money management becomes, because it can make the difference between just surviving and living in a way that enables you to reward yourself with things you enjoy. Mastering the skills of becoming a successful money manager leads to better control over money and other areas of your life as well. The investment of time you make in mastering these skills will pay off for you in many ways.

CAN THE AVERAGE PERSON REALLY BECOME A MILLIONAIRE?

There are more opportunities today to become a millionaire than there ever were. High technology has opened unlimited markets. Every day, people who are average and who have developed an idea that works join the ranks of the millionaires. But be careful not to seek something you may not really want. You don't have to be a millionaire to enjoy life. People who spend their life trying to become millionaires usually have a more difficult time than people who spend their life doing what they enjoy doing. Pay yourself daily rewards. Enjoy life. Provide something worthwhile to other people and you will rise slowly to your level of performance. Life can be a rich, rewarding experience with or without a lot of money. Use the *millionaire's attitude* to live life as if you were a millionaire, and you can have the best of both worlds.

HOW TO AVOID FAMILY MONEY ARGUMENTS

The "power of the purse" has caused family arguments, royal conflicts, wars, and unrest since the beginning of recorded history.

Today, just as in the past, arguments about money often escalate into the most explosive and unpleasant experiences a family can have. In many cases, money isn't the real issue at all; it's just the excuse for letting off steam. There may be other problems, repressed emotions, and conflicts in a family which surface around an argument over money.

There are a number of techniques a family can use to reduce the chance of this kind of argument happening. Review the following techniques and practice them until you find some that work for you and your family.

1. LIMIT THE AMOUNT OF MONEY YOU WILL ARGUE ABOUT

You can avoid many unpleasant family money arguments by establishing a minimum amount of money you will agree to argue about. For example, you may determine that you will not argue about an expense under $25. By setting this kind of a limit, you automatically eliminate petty expenditures as a cause of argument.

You should set a reasonable minimum limit that fits the plans you have worked out together as a family to achieve your financial objectives. If, after setting these minimum limits, you still continue to argue over small amounts of money, the chances are that you are not arguing over money but using money to surface other problems you may be having.

2. UNDERSTAND WHAT YOU ARE ARGUING ABOUT

Be sure that what is starting out as an argument or a fight is truly related to a money matter. Often people pick money issues to fight over because they are concrete examples of something that isn't going well, but in reality there are other subjects that surface through an apparent concern about a financial issue. So be sure to ask yourself: Is this argument really about money?

Arguments escalate into fights and battles as the degree of emotional intensity increases. Be sure to take a look at your problem-solving style to see if you can modify it to avoid tension and frustration when you do discuss money matters with other people.

It is often more important *how* you deal with an argument or a fight than it is whether you have an argument or a fight. Try to keep from escalating money discussions into arguments or fights, but if this happens, be sure to develop a means to defuse the situation of its potential danger to your relationship with the people around you.

SO IN GENERAL . . .

- Don't let a problem situation creep up on you and take you by surprise. Try to keep an eye on what is happening with the other people in your family as to family money matters. Have regular discussion sessions about your family money objectives. Update the state of your family financial situation. (Make sure everyone really understands where you are.) Anticipate rough spots that might be coming up between you and others. Open up a flow of communications early on.
- Exchange ideas, thoughts, feelings, needs, and wants as they relate to money matters. Find out where you stand with other people in relation to money. Take time to talk when the pressure is off.
- Money is a big source of potential security in our society, and a threat—real or imagined—to its existence creates tension and anxiety for people. The more clarity and openness you can foster for people, the less threatening the total environment will be. Misunderstandings, which can lead to arguments or fights, can be headed off by getting a lot of information on the table early, including what your *ideas* and *feelings* about money in a particular situation may be. Avoid misunderstandings by opening the door to communications through talking and discussing what's happening all the way along the path of a financial relationship with another person.
- But if an argument does get started, in order to avoid fights . . . try not to push the other person into a corner by telling them what they are doing wrong in the situation. Talk about what your feelings are toward yourself and about what *you* are up to.

Focus on your own feelings, thoughts, concerns, ideas, and plans.

- If you feel you are not being heard by the other person ask them for a statement of what they think you are trying to say. Get clarification right away about how you are being received.
- Write down details when you are receiving information so you can be accurate about what you think is taking place in the discussion, argument, or fight. Repeat back what you think you are hearing. This gives both you and the other person a sense of order and the feeling that you care about what is taking place.
- Don't be reluctant to be friendly during one of these sessions. Take a minute out to make a friendly gesture or comment even if it's not directly related to the immediate issue. Joke a little.
- Try to stick closely to the main issue that has come up. Avoid bringing into the discussion all your complaints from the past and dumping them on the other person as soon as the discussion temperature rises.
- Try to "agree to disagree." That is, try to establish that it is OK not to agree with each other. You may have different points of view and that is OK. This will only really work if you develop an ability to have it be OK to *lose an argument.* Learn the magic phrase: "I hear what you are saying although I don't agree with you. I think that . . ."
- Don't spend a long time in the process of the argument. Take a physical break and get a breath of fresh air, some food, or even agree to take the rest of the day off from the discussion.

- You may have to stop the discussion, argument or fight even though the other person doesn't want to do so. This can be a really difficult thing to do. When you determine you have reached the limit of your ability to concentrate and remain in control of your emotions, you must stop the exchange. When you decide this point is coming up, let the other person know a little bit in advance so that you don't cut him or her off abruptly. Tell them that you are going to want to stop the discussion and then, after giving them time to respond, *stop it.* This may include your having to leave the room and literally stop the session by getting out of the immediate area. This is not "copping out." When you reach a point where you are no longer able to process the information being exchanged, it is time to break off the communication. It's time for both your brains to work on the input. Give the subject some time so that you can digest what has been communicated between you.

- Avoid meal times and late night sessions whenever possible. You are least able to function calmly on an empty stomach.

- If there has been a lot of drinking going on, you should avoid getting into a heavy discussion, an argument, or a fight. Drinking does not produce a constructive environment for exchanging information. Have fun instead at these times, and reserve your discussions for later.

- Don't sandbag the other person by saving up the clincher to your point of view until the very end of the argument—like dropping a big bomb. Get your real ideas and feelings out as soon as you can identify them.

- After a session has terminated, make some arrangements to take time to review what went on during the session and how you have come to feel about it later on—the next day for instance.

- An ounce of prevention . . . But again, don't wait until the trouble starts up again or the frustration mounts to the point where a fight is the only recourse to release the tension, to clear the air, or to reopen your communications with the other person.

- Review your financial situation regularly. Anticipate a financial crisis before it occurs. Deal little by little to avoid the big surprise which comes like a shock and startles everyone.

- Discover what your pattern is in the process of having a discussion, argument, fight, or battle which relates to money. Know in advance what you are up to so you can work toward de-escalating a potentially dangerous situation along the way. You won't always avoid the escalation of a discussion into an argument or a fight, but you can develop techniques to stop it in motion or avoid its getting worse.

- Ask yourself what role you usually play in an argument about money—the boss, the victim, the pacifier, the one who escalates, the keeper of the records, the misunderstood one, the person who never gets what you want, the good guy, etc.

- It's all in the family . . . Find out what each person in your family needs or wants to know about money. Do not assume that you always know what each member of your family thinks about money. Let them tell you. Do you have discussions about money or is it a secret area in your family? Who has what fears or apprehensions about money in your family? How are these fears managed in your family?

- Get each family member's notions about money out into the open. See if there are any inaccurate ideas which might require clearing up.

- Don't protect your family from knowing about how much money is earned in your household and how it is spent. A discussion of your family money goals can set the stage for the prevention of misunderstandings about money later on and give all the family a sense of participation in the money management process.

- Be realistic about what money is available for the family to use.

- Don't use the availability of money as a weapon or scare tactic to control the other members of your family. Allowances, for example, are given because by giving one, you are helping someone achieve a sense of autonomy who might not otherwise be able to come up with the money to be independent. Don't attach strings to this kind of a gift and don't give an allowance if you can't realistically afford to do so, because you'll end up resenting it and looking for rewards or behaviors that will make the other person *less* independent.

- Don't confuse paying members of your own family to do work for you with the notion that you are doing them a favor by providing such income. Pay them because it is worth it to you to get the work done. Don't hold it against that person if they don't want to do a job for you. Allow them to decide whether they want to work for you or not. Avoid saying, "How come you were willing to mow the lawn last week but won't do it today?" This approach to money management doesn't really teach anything to anyone. It creates guilt. Don't try to educate or teach responsibility with money. If you do, money will then be associated with work in too rigid a way and can develop negative attitudes about work in the other members of your family.

SUMMARY

Fear is a basic ingredient that can produce apprehension, tension, anxiety, and anger, which can result in upset feelings, outbursts, arguments, and battles. By sharing your money goals with the rest of your family, and by communicating together regularly about each of your money needs, you can build a creative and positive team. Together you can share the joy of achieving your family financial goals and also share the burden of the struggle, if or when things go wrong financially. All of us need to know that someone else cares about our own needs. By following the techniques suggested in this program, you can successfully put money to work for you and generate harmony in your family.

HOW TO DEAL WITH A MONEY CRISIS

As inflation continues to increase the price of goods and services, it is possible that you and your family may find yourselves in a money crisis at one time or another. The crisis may occur for a number of reasons:

1. You or your spouse may lose your job.
2. You may incur medical/hospital bills over and above your insurance coverage.
3. You may have overextended your credit.
4. You or your spouse may die and leave an estate insufficient to cover the needs of your family.
5. You may have invested in something that went sour and left you with enormous debts.
6. You may be living above the financial level you can realistically afford.

There is often some temporary solution to a money crisis caused by either the loss of a job or overextended credit. For example, you might be able to solve the crisis by:

1. Taking out a bank loan.
2. Borrowing against your life insurance policy.
3. Borrowing against other equity (the equity on your home, etc.).
4. Receiving unemployment benefits (or, in extreme cases, welfare).

However, the death of the principal wage earner in the family or the extreme loss you might take on an investment gone bad will require a reevaluation of your family priorities and a definite change in the family life-style.

In many cases, this may be only the first step toward finding a solution to the problem. The financial crisis may continue for a prolonged period of time. You may find bills piling up and be unable to pay them. This may lead to the involvement of a collection agency. When a family's credit capabilities are totally exhausted, the financial situation may be further complicated by garnished earnings, repossessed autos and/or furnishings, and small claims court judgments.

Unless you have developed a strategy for dealing with this kind of stress, life may become extremely unpleasant for you and your family. By using the techniques suggested in this program, you and your family can develop money management plans that can bring you back from a serious financial crisis. If your creditors believe you are seriously working to repay your obligations, you have a good chance of working things out. There are a number of important psychological strategies you can use to deal with the stresses which usually result from suffering through a financial crisis. The following techniques should give you the means that you and your family can use to reduce the pressures you will be working against while you solve your financial problems:

- Avoid getting into a state of extreme agitation or panic. Don't generalize too much. Don't predict doom or try to predict too far into the future. Put the problem in perspective, step by step. In times of crisis, it is better to plan life day by day.

- Take care of your physical health. The tension levels will be higher than usual so you will need rest, food, and a minimum of stimulants. Don't upset your usual routines for taking good care of your health. Try not to get into problem-solving sessions around dinnertime or late at night (i.e., low energy times).

- In addition to the general process of staying healthy, try to keep up a pattern of getting out and having some entertainment. Keep your appointments. Maintain your contact with family and friends.

- Set up some times to work on your financial problems. Create a schedule for dealing with events on your own terms. This way you won't carry around as much of a concern about what you are going to do.

- Avoid setting up a pattern of trying to find fault or placing the blame on other people for your problem. Don't look back. Instead, see what it is you can do to work out solutions. Don't blame anyone, *especially* yourself, for what has happened. Save your energy.

- Begin to list all the possible solutions or alternatives to your problem. Write down the pros and cons of all the alternatives. Get them in a form that you can see, and save your work even when you change your strategies. It is important to see where you have been and to see that you have been able to come up with some ideas. You are not helpless.

- Begin to take action step by step on the ideas, solutions, directions, and action steps you have developed. Be sure to do a little something each day and review what you have done.

- Let other people know what you are up to. Don't avoid letting close friends and family know about the financial difficulties you are having. This doesn't necessarily mean that you are asking them for help (or you might want to do so which is OK), but it is important that you do not isolate yourself and cut off the contact you enjoy with other people. Don't go underground to save face. Doing so only creates more tension and anxiety, which can lead to more panic. Keep open to the people around you.

- Include your total immediate family or roommates or close friends at some level in the process of solving your financial problem. Let them participate to some degree if they want to. Ask them if they have time to listen and discuss your problem. Keep looking for good ideas from every source.

- When dealing with creditors, bankers, etc., don't be overly pessimistic or optimistic. Try to give and get a realistic and accurate picture of your situation.

- When talking with others whom you have decided you want to include in the situation, be sure to let them know some of your feelings about what is taking place. It's OK to say you're a little worried or tense or upset. It's OK to have a problem. When things turn around, be sure to let these people know the steps you have taken to improve your financial situation.

- Don't try to resolve your problem in one sitting. It's

good to have an overview, but you need to allow time and space to get relevant information. Seek out and ask questions to the right people (specialists such as bankers, attorneys, brokers, psychologists, etc.). Try out various alternatives. Keep a balance in your life. Maintain good energy.

MONEY CRISIS PRACTICE EXERCISE

When you are facing a money crisis, take time to go through the following steps before you charge ahead into action:

- Write out a list of people you might call if a money crisis has occurred in your life.
- What would you tell each one of them? Practice running through a session with your husband/wife, children, mother, best friend, etc. Imagine talking to each one of them. How might it go? What would you say? How would they respond? What fears might your financial problem, if any, raise in their minds?
- Make a list of your feelings about what you would want to handle alone and what you might want to talk to other people about.
- See if you can recall the last time a money crisis came into your life. What was it like? How did you feel? What were your patterns of thinking and behavior during that stress period?

WHAT ABOUT FILING FOR BANKRUPTCY?

In some cases, in spite of the action steps you take to solve a financial crisis, you may be forced to consider bankruptcy.

When your family debts reach the point where it is extremely unlikely that you can repay them over a three-year period based on current earnings, or when your family credit has been exceeded or exhausted, voluntary bankruptcy should be considered as an alternative solution to your financial problem. If you reach this state of extreme financial difficulty, the principal wage earner may have no choice, because creditors will probably force a bankruptcy hearing.

In general, bankruptcy laws have been set up with the intention of offering an individual an opportunity to start over. When considering bankruptcy, however, you should consider the shattering, devastating effect it can have on you and your family's morale and credibility. Regardless of what you may have been told, the process of filing for bankruptcy and being so adjudicated is extremely difficult for some people to endure, and it must therefore be considered only in extreme cases. It is also important to remember that in some states, if both the husband and wife are signatories on applications for credit which has been extended, they are separately liable for the entire amount owed. It may be necessary, therefore, for both parties to file for bankruptcy. Failure to do so by both signatories may result in your family finding itself owing some of the exact same bills after the principal wage earner has gone through the entire bankruptcy process.

There are quite a few questions to be dealt with prior to filing for bankruptcy, such as:

1. Can you keep your home?
2. Can you keep your car?

3. Can any furniture be returned?
4. Where must you put savings or cash to protect it?
5. How much of your cash and savings can be protected?
6. Must you lose equipment such as power tools, etc.?
7. What happens to your musical instruments, works of art, jewelry, etc.?

Bankruptcy is a difficult, emotionally draining process and should never be attempted without proper legal counsel. In most metropolitan areas there are attorneys who specialize in bankruptcy. Your private attorney will be happy to refer you to such a specialist. If you have no private attorney, seek the assistance of your local Legal Aid Society. Above all, *never attempt to go through bankruptcy yourself.*

CONCLUSION

Facing a money crisis can be a devastating experience or an opportunity for growth. Throughout history, millions of people from all walks of life have run into financial difficulties. Those people who retained their sense of values and attacked the money crisis problem with the same spirit of adventure and optimism with which they met other challenges in their lives, generally worked their way out of their problems.

You will do much better in meeting a financial crisis by involving other people (your friends, family, etc.) in your problem. By sharing your problem, you open up opportunities for solutions. You have other people in your corner. Don't hide your problem or try to keep up the appearance that it doesn't exist. You are looking for the truth and there is no dishonor in facing a financial crisis head on and taking the necessary steps to cut your expenses and get back on your feet.

Money is only a part of life. As you master the skills of successful money management, you will be able to control your financial future to a much greater degree.

INVESTMENT CHECK-OFF LIST

What follows is a very generalized review of various investment opportunities available today. Before you make any investment, you should take time to thoroughly learn the particular *investment game* you are getting into. Then you should seek out the most reputable specialist you can hire to protect you and your investment.

The objective of this investment list is simply to provide you with a way to become familiar with some of the investment terms being used today. The Investment Chart which follows the Investment Definitions will give you a very general idea as to the cost, type of return, and time required to make the investment pay off (i.e., how long you usually have to leave your money in the investment).

INVESTMENT DEFINITIONS

The following investments are listed in the order most people find themselves investing: Savings accounts and insurance appear first and the more sophisticated investments come along later (bonds, second mortgages, etc.).

1. INVESTMENT

Money investments are things you place your money into because you want to earn money on your money. An investment succeeds when you earn money on your money and are able to sell the investment for at least as much or more than you paid for it.

Investment return usually comes back to you as money paid to you or as the increased value of your investment over what you paid for it.

There are two primary kinds of investments:

a. Fixed investments, which pay a fixed amount of interest on your money (bank savings accounts, mortgages, etc.).
b. Variable investments, which fluctuate in the amount you are paid back depending on the value of the investment at the time you sell it (e.g., stocks, real estate, etc.)

You should tailor your investments to your own life-style and particular financial needs. Generally you are looking for safety, liquidity, and convenience when you consider an investment. The lower the risk of the investment, the lower return you will usually get.

2. SAVINGS ACCOUNTS

Banks, saving and loan associations, credit unions, etc., provide you with a means to lend out your money. In return they pay you a fixed amount of interest. Most of these investments are very safe and insured by the federal government. Your investment return will be generally low, with a slightly higher return on long-term deposits (called certificates of deposit) in which you agree to leave your money for a minimum term of one year, three years, or longer.

Your investment receipt is your savings passbook or your monthly or quarterly statement.

3. INSURANCE

You will most likely want to invest in a life insurance policy of some kind. The younger you are, the less you will have to pay over the years for your insurance. Insurance protects you and your family against death while at the same time setting up a *forced savings program* that can pay you attractive dividends over the long term as well as tax advantages in retirement annuities. Insurance is becoming an extremely complex field and your best approach is to find out who the brightest, sharpest, most up-to-date insurance broker is in your community, and call to set up an appointment.

4. REAL ESTATE (YOUR HOME, CONDOMINIUM, ETC.)

An investment in your own home can be one of the best investments, because you are combining a very real personal need with an investment that pays you tax benefits as well as inflation hedges. Your best bet is not to overextend yourself. Look for a smaller home in a good neighborhood that you can improve while you live there. Use a bright, knowledgeable real-estate broker to help you find the house you want. Be patient and don't pay the asking price. Shop around until you get the chance to buy what you want under the market price.

5. MUTUAL FUNDS

When you begin to generate surplus capital over and above money you need in your savings account, you may want to consider investing in stocks. In the beginning, when you have a limited amount to invest, you can use a mutual fund. Mutual funds allow you to make a fixed investment each month so that you are putting your money into stocks instead of into a savings account.

The incentive to do this is that inflation (the reduction in the value of your money because of rising prices) reduces the value of your balance in a savings account if the interest you're being paid does not equal the rate of inflationary increase. When you invest in stocks, you have the opportunity to benefit from the increased prices of the stock due to either inflation or to growth and profitability of the company.

You can select a conservative mutual fund and track your investment over a period of months to see how you are doing. Before getting into the stock market, you should take time to study it thoroughly and you should find yourself a stock broker of unquestioned integrity and ability.

6. STOCKS

Stocks are shares of ownership in a business. The two basic kinds of stocks are common stock and preferred stock. Preferred stockholders are paid first and the risk is less than it is for common stock. Common stockholders are paid dividends depending on the profitability of the company that has been invested in. Your receipt for this investment is a stock certificate.

You should thoroughly understand what you are doing before you invest in the stock market. The long-term return you receive on your stock investments will depend primarily on how much you learn about the stock investment game. Debentures are a kind of stock secured by company assets with a fixed rate of return. Debentures are closer to loans than common stock and therefore usually pay less of a return.

7. BONDS

Bonds are simply a means the government and companies use to borrow your money. Your bond certificate is your receipt that over a given period of time you will be paid a fixed rate of interest, and at the end of the period of time you will be paid your original investment back.

Bonds are conservative investments and generally pay a low to moderate rate of return. Government bonds are extremely safe investments. Because of tax considerations, investments in municipals (local government bonds) often become important to people in higher tax brackets.

You will want to understand the bond market before you become involved in investing in it.

8. REAL ESTATE (INCOME PROPERTY)

Raw land, rental property, etc., can be a good investment for you. The advantage of this kind of investment is that you can often invest in your own community and control your investment yourself. Many people today are forming investment groups with friends and buying income property together.

You will want to study the real estate market and understand it before you become involved in real estate investments. If you are handy with tools and like to paint, investing in income property can be rewarding financially as well as psychologically. Since the beginning of time people have enjoyed the feeling of owning property. As a landlord, you can physically see your investment, improve it, and enjoy it.

9. REAL ESTATE (SECOND MORTGAGES)

A second mortgage is a loan against a home or an income property which is subordinated to the first mortgage. This means that should the person who is paying off the mortgage default (i.e., be unable to pay), the holder of the first mortgage is paid off first through the sale of the property.

There are advantages and disadvantages to holding second mortgages. Before getting into this investment you will want to thoroughly understand what you are doing. Second mortgages can give you an opportunity to make a higher return on your money with relatively low risk.

10. REAL PROPERTY (COLLECTOR'S ITEMS, ANTIQUES, STAMPS, ETC.)

There are many areas in which markets are established by collectors. Each is different, and returns vary widely. Though the payoff on this kind of investment is often extremely long term, this kind of an investment can be the most rewarding one you make.

This is true because you can invest in something that you enjoy. If you are by nature a collector, you can have years of fun while steadily increasing your holdings.

11. BUSINESS VENTURES

You may decide to go into business for yourself on a part-time or full-time basis.

Your success will depend on your abilities, drive, management skills, luck, and a number of other things. You can't go wrong investing in yourself. But at the same time, new business ventures have the highest mortality rate of just about anything around.

Your best approach is to be patient. Start slowly and limit your risks. Let the marketplace tell you whether it looks like you can make a go of whatever it is you want to do.

The best hedge against failure in this investment area is to plan, plan, plan, and use other people's money to test your concepts. Be prepared for months or years of long, hard hours. But if it's what you want to do, perhaps nothing can be more satisfying than working for yourself and watching a business you built from scratch prosper as it provides services or products to other people.

12. TAX SHELTERS

Your best bet is to avoid investments you don't understand. By hiring a reputable CPA and tax attorney and by investing in yourself, you should be able to find imaginative ways to invest your money without having to invest in strange deals such as oil wells, Hollywood movies, cattle, or commodities in Brazil if you are unfamiliar with these industries.

Many a person has lost everything trying to keep from paying income taxes.

13. GOLD

Lately, gold has become the rage. Gold is a commodity. When you put money into commodities, you are not investing—you are speculating. Speculating means that you are *guessing* which way the future markets will go.

You won't go wrong by thinking of gold and commodities as gambling opportunities. If you like to gamble, great! Gamble away, but don't confuse yourself by thinking you are investing.

INVESTMENT CHART

Review the following Investment Chart to give yourself a general idea of the kind of investment opportunities that are out there waiting for your money.

Investment Chart

TYPE	DESCRIPTION	COST	% RETURN	TERM
Bank, Savings & Loan, etc.	1. Savings Acct's. 2. Certif-icates	None None	Low Low (+)	Daily Return Varies
Life Insurance	1. Ordinary 2. Endowment 3. Single Premium 4. Annuities	Low/ Moderate Moderate High Moderate	Moderate Moderate Moderate Moderate/ Low	Long Term Long Term Long Term Long Term
Real Estate	1. Home/Con-dominium	High	Moderate/ High	Moderate/ Long Term
Stocks/Bonds	1. Mutual Funds 2. Stocks 3. Bonds/Cor-porate 4. Bonds/U.S. Gov't. 5. Bonds/Mu-nicipal	None/ Low Low/ Moderate Moderate Low Low/ Moderate	Varies Varies Moderate Low Moderate	Moderate Moderate Moderate/ Long Term Moderate/ Long Term Moderate/ Long Term
Real Estate	1. Income Property 2. Apartment Bldgs.	High High	Moderate High	Moderate Immediate
Real Property	1. Works of Art 2. Antiques 3. Collec-tions	High High Varies	Moderate/ High Moderate Varies	Moderate/ Long Term Moderate Varies
Business Ventures	1. Small Business 2. Entertain-ment 3. New Cor-porations	High High High	Varies Varies Varies	Varies Short Term Moderate/ Long Term

REINFORCEMENT POINTS

Each of these points contains a specific money management technique designed to help you master control over your money. Review them daily or select a single point each day. Concentrate on practicing each technique until you *automatically* master control over your money.

1. USE THE MAGIC WORD, "NO"

NO is the most powerful word you can use to control the flow of your money. Use it to keep from impulse buying or to keep from getting into situations you don't want to be in. Practice saying "no" to yourself so that you are not always reacting to what other people suggest. Practice saying "no" to other people.

2. CONTROL YOUR EXPENSES

Review your daily expenses to make sure your money isn't being nickeled and dimed away. Resist impulse buying. Don't use credit for luxury items. Plan ahead for your vacations. Make a game out of saving money. At the end of the day take all your loose change and put it into a bank. See how fast it begins to grow. Seek out ways to entertain yourself that don't cost money.

3. RIDE YOUR WINNERS

When you find something going well for you, keep going as long as it pays off for you. Start small and build up your investments as you learn to play the money game. Be patient. Find a winning game and keep playing it. Cut your losses short and don't look back.

4. FAIL SUCCESSFULLY

Don't be afraid to fail. Don't waste energy trying to cover up failure. Learn from your failures and go on to the next challenge. It's OK to fail. If you're not failing, you're not growing. Fail successfully. Use your failures to become more experienced and more effective.

5. PICTURE WHAT IT IS YOU WANT

Make a list of your financial goals. Visualize your having them. Don't worry about *how* you will get them. Cut out pictures from magazines which illustrate what it is you want (a new car, a big house, beautiful clothes). Practice actually seeing, feeling, and tasting the things you want to come into your life.

6. DON'T GO UNDERGROUND

When you are facing a serious financial crisis don't try to hide it from close friends and family. Share your problem. Ask other people to give you ideas. Accept the reality of your situation. Let others know if you need help. Keep yourself out in the open and attack the problem with energy and positive optimism.

7. LIVE WITHIN YOUR INCOME

Don't overextend yourself to appear to have more money than you really have. Enjoy whatever money you have. Keep your expenses below your income. Use your imagination to entertain yourself. Don't try to fool other people because you will only end up fooling yourself.

8. THINK TODAY

Try not to let past failures inhibit you. Don't spend so much time in the future that you ignore the present. Live in the now of your life. Experience what is happening to you today, good or bad. Living *one day at a time* enriches your experience and turns your future into a present you can control. Today is here and offers you an opportunity to do something right now.

9. USE THE MILLIONAIRE'S ATTITUDE

Don't let money or the lack of it deaden your natural spirit. Enjoy your life. Accept it. Refuse to envy people who *appear* to have more wealth than you do. Seek out experiences you enjoy and avoid unpleasant people who clutter up your life. Put money in its place once and for all as something you control to work for you.

10. CUT YOUR LOSSES SHORT

If you've got yourself into a losing situation, cut your losses immediately. If you've miscalculated, made a mistake, or failed, admit it and take your losses and go on to the next challenge. Nothing drains away more energy than continuing to follow a plan you no longer believe in. It's far better to take your losses than to go on trying to make an unworkable investment work.

11. PAY YOUR TAXES

Take every legitimate deduction you can but don't get yourself involved in intricate tax shelter deals you don't understand. Pay an expert to do your tax returns for you. Use successful money management to control your expenses and stretch the value of the money you have left over after taxes.

12. DON'T PANIC!

When a money crisis hits you, don't panic. Millions of people throughout history have had to face sudden financial reverses. Keep calm and take time to work your way out of your financial problems. Don't try to project forward what may happen. Don't worry about the downside results. Keep working away at your problems until you begin to create solutions.

13. REWARD YOURSELF

Pay yourself daily rewards whatever the results. Don't be too hard on yourself. Enjoy life. Relax. Step back from what you are doing and concentrate on the process of living. Set small rewards to look forward to each week. Live in the present and reward yourself now.

14. USE TEACUP ECONOMICS TO KEEP EXPENSES IN LINE

Pay yourself first. Pay all your bills. Put away emergency money. Deduct all your known expenses from your paycheck on the first of each month. Then use what is left over for entertainment. Learn how to say, "I'm sorry but I can't afford to do that this month."

15. PAY FOR FINANCIAL SPECIALISTS

The best investment you can make is an investment in yourself. The next best investment is in the specialists you can hire to advise you on your investments. It costs a little more, but every penny is worth it. The grief, losses, and trouble you will save are well worth the expense. Only amateurs try to do things in areas in which they are unqualified. Professionals pay professionals to get the job done right.

16. CONTROL YOUR APPETITES

Learn to moderate your living so that you don't burn out your natural energy supplies. Excess generally distorts your life patterns both physically and emotionally. A moderate, healthy pattern of exercise, food, sleep, and relaxation goes a long way to providing you with the level of energy you need for personal problem solving.

17. ASK THE MAGIC QUESTION, "WHY?"

Don't do things automatically. Ask yourself why you need to buy what you are buying. Why does it have to be new? Why can't I get along without it? Why am I spending this money? Keep asking yourself "why" until you have really analyzed what it is you are really doing and why you are really doing it.

18. LOOK THROUGH MONEY

Don't let money get in your way. Look through money to the things you really want to do. Concentrate on the real objectives you are after. Experience the real-world payoffs you are seeking. Are you sure you can't get what you really want without having to spend a lot of money? Live your life. Use money to support your plans for your life. Be careful not to use your life to earn money.

19. INVEST IN YOURSELF

The best investment you can make is in yourself. Invest in your own dreams, plans, skills, desires, hopes, and fantasies. The richness of your life will result from what you put into it. Keep learning and growing all your life. Use your money to increase your awareness and your capacity to enjoy the gift of life. A trip to Europe is often a much better investment than another $1,500 in your savings account.

INDEX